CUTTING
EDGE

STARTER

STUDENTS' BOOK

sarah cunningham   **chris redston**
with peter moor

PEARSON
Longman

Module	Grammar	Vocabulary	Reading and Listening
Module 1 Nice to meet you **page 6** *Do you remember?* page 13	1) *I/my* and *you/your*: (*my name's .../I'm .../What's your name?*) 2) *he/she* and *his/her*: (*What's his job? What's her name? Her name's ... He's a ...*) *Pronunciation*: sentence stress and word stress	**Vocabulary:** jobs and *a/an*; numbers 0–20; the alphabet; *How do you spell ...?* [TB] **Vocabulary booster:** jobs	**Reading:** personal information – names [WB] **Listen and read:** *Real names*
Module 2 Around the world **page 14** *Do you remember?* page 21	1) *be* with *I* and *you* (affirmative, questions and negative) 2) *be* with *he*, *she* and *it* (affirmative, questions and negative) *Pronunciation*: word stress, contracted verb forms and sentence stress	**Vocabulary:** countries and nationalities; numbers: 21–100 [TB] **Vocabulary booster:** nationalities	**Listening:** listening for personal information [WB] **Listen and read:** *Where in the world ... ?*
Module 3 In a different country **page 22** *Do you remember?* page 29	1) *be* – plural forms; *our* and *their* 2) **plural nouns** 3) *this/that/these/those* *Pronunciation*: plural nouns and contracted verb forms	**Vocabulary:** places; food and drink; common adjectives [TB] **Vocabulary booster:** food and drink	**Reading:** an email and a postcard [WB] **Listen and read:** *Eating and drinking around the world*
Module 4 Around town **page 30** *Do you remember?* page 37	1) *there is/there are* (affirmative, questions and negative) 2) *a*, *some* and *any* *Pronunciation*: /ð/ and /θ/; sentence stress	**Vocabulary:** places in a town; prepositions of place; common adjectives [TB] **Vocabulary booster:** places in a town/city	**Listening:** descriptions of a place **Reading:** My home town [WB] **Listen and read:** *The World Showcase*

Consolidation Modules 1–4 (pages 38–39)

Module	Grammar	Vocabulary	Reading and Listening
Module 5 Home, work and family **page 40** *Do you remember?* page 47	1) Present Simple with *I* and *you* (affirmative, questions and negative) 2) possessive *'s* *Pronunciation*: possessive *'s* and sentence stress	**Vocabulary:** family members; personal possessions [TB] **Vocabulary booster:** rooms in the house	**Reading:** three people **Listening:** complete a form [WB] **Listen and read:** *Facts and figures*
Module 6 We both like ... **page 48** *Do you remember?* page 55	1) Present Simple with *he*, *she* and *it* (affirmative, questions and negative) 2) Object pronouns *Pronunciation*: Present Simple verb forms	**Vocabulary:** likes and dislikes; free time activities [TB] **Vocabulary booster:** sports	**Listening:** lifestyle facts **Reading:** likes and dislikes [WB] **Listen and read:** *Famous couples*

[TB] Exercises to be found in the Teacher's Resource Book   [WB] Exercises to be found in the Workbook

Speaking task	Writing	Real Life
Preparation for task: listen to questions requesting personal information **Task:** complete forms with students' full names	[WB] **Improve your writing:** full stops (.) and question marks (?) [WB] **Punctuation:** capital letters (1)	**Real life:** greetings – saying *hello* and *goodbye*; classroom language
Preparation for task: listen to someone talk about her friends and complete the information **Task:** talk about your friends and ask questions about your partner's friends	**Writing:** fill in a form [WB] **Improve your writing:** write about yourself [WB] **Punctuation:** capital letters (2)	**Real life:** phone numbers, filling in a form *Pronunciation:* sentence stress in questions
Preparation for task: look at a café menu and write a conversation **Task:** act the conversation for the class	[WB] **Improve your writing:** a postcard	**Real life:** ordering and paying for food and drink in a café; prices
Preparation for tasks: 1) make sentences to describe a picture; 2) write ten questions about where another student lives **Tasks:** 1) find eight differences between two pictures; 2) interview a student about where he/she lives	**Writing:** write a paragraph about where you live [WB] **Improve your writing:** capital letters (revision)	**Real life:** In the street *Pronunciation:* sentence stress
Preparation for task: write about members of your family **Task:** talk about your family with another student	**Writing:** write about yourself [WB] **Improve your writing:** write about your family [WB] **Writing:** prepositions; articles	**Real life:** buying things in shops
Preparation for tasks: ask questions about other students' likes and dislikes **Tasks:** talk about the likes and dislikes of the class	[WB] **Improve your writing:** using pronouns	**Real life:** telling the time (1)

Module	Grammar	Vocabulary	Reading and Listening
Module 7 Your time **page 56** *Do you remember?* **page 63**	**Present Simple with adverbs of frequency** *Pronunciation:* word stress – days of the week	Vocabulary: daily routines; time expressions; days of the week TB **Vocabulary booster:** *verbs and nouns*	Reading: unusual routines Listening: *In my country ...* WB **Listen and read:** Life in Britain today
Module 8 People are amazing **page 64** *Do you remember?* **page 71**	1) *Can* and *can't* for ability 2) *Wh-* Questions *Pronunciation: can* and *can't;* word stress – quantities	Vocabulary: parts of the body; quantities TB **Vocabulary booster:** parts of the body	Reading and listening: *You're amazing* WB **Listen and read:** *Living in the Antarctic*

Consolidation Modules 5–8 (pages 72–73)

Module	Grammar	Vocabulary	Reading and Listening
Module 9 Now and then **page 74** *Do you remember?* **page 81**	**Past Simple of** *be* **(affirmative, questions and negative)** *Pronunciation: was/wasn't* and *were/weren't*	Vocabulary: common adjectives TB **Vocabulary booster:** adjectives for describing people	Reading and listening: facts about 1900 Reading: *born in 1900* WB **Listen and read:** *When they were young*
Module 10 Creative people **page 82** *Do you remember?* **page 89**	**Past Simple of regular verbs and some common irregular ones (affirmative sentences)** *Pronunciation:* regular and irregular past verb forms; word stress – months	Vocabulary: life events; dates TB **Vocabulary booster:** more common irregular verbs	Reading: *The Writer and the Wizard* Reading and listening: King Arthur WB **Listen and read:** *the Kennedys*
Module 11 Going away **page 90** *Do you remember?* **page 97**	1) Past Simple negative 2) Past Simple questions (*yes/no* questions and *Wh-* questions) 3) *and* and *but*	Vocabulary: holiday expressions; irregular verbs TB **Vocabulary booster:** the weather	Reading: *The family who sailed round the world* Listening: holiday in the USA WB **Listen and read:** *Holiday destinations*
Module 12 Spending money **page 98** *Do you remember?* **page 105**	1) *want to* 2) *going to* future *Pronunciation:* sentence stress; weak form of *to*	Vocabulary: things you buy; colours and sizes TB **Vocabulary booster:** clothes	Reading: *websites* WB **Listen and read:** *AIBO the electronic pet*

Consolidation Modules 9–12 (pages 106–107)

Communication activities (pages 108–112)

Speaking task	Writing	Real Life
Preparation for tasks: 1) decide on your daily routine; 2) write questions to interview your teacher **Tasks:** 1) ask another student about his/her routine; 2) interview your teacher	**Writing:** write about your daily routine and free time [WB] **Improve your writing:** personal descriptions [WB] **Spelling:** double letters	**Real life:** telling the time (2); talking about TV programmes
Preparation for task: listen to two people discussing what they can and can't do **Task:** compare things you and your partner can and can't do	**Writing:** the first seven years [WB] **Improve your writing:** describe yourself [WB] **Spelling:** 'silent' letters	**Real life:** big numbers
Preparation for task: write answers to ask another student about his/her childhood **Task:** interview your partner about his/her childhood	[WB] **Improve your writing:** write about the past [WB] **Writing:** contractions	**Real life:** years and ages
Preparation for task: produce a time line for your life **Task:** talk about your life events	**Writing:** creative people [WB] **Improve your writing:** a personal history	**Real life:** months and dates
Preparation for task: write questions about the past to ask other students **Task:** play a board game using Past Simple questions	**Writing:** make sentences with *and* and *but* [WB] **Improve your writing:** write an email	**Real life:** buying a train ticket
Preparation for task: write questions to ask other students about next weekend **Task:** ask and answer questions about next weekend and report back to the class	**Writing:** write sentences about things you want/don't want to do [WB] **Improve your writing:** punctuation and capital letters	**Real life:** best wishes for the future

(**Language summary** (pages 113–118))   (**Tapescripts** (pages 119–127))

module 1

Nice to meet you

▶ **Grammar:** *I/my, you/your, he/his, she/her, a/an*
▶ **Vocabulary:** jobs; the alphabet; *How do you spell ... ?;* numbers 0–20
▶ **Real life:** *hello* and *goodbye;* classroom language

Hello, are you David?

Yes ...

Hi, I'm Rosa.

Hello, Rosa. Nice to meet you!

What's your name?

Hi, my name's Ebru Kemal, and I'm a student.

Hello, I'm Jim Kendler, and I'm your teacher.

Focus 1

Names and introductions

1 ▭ [1.1] Look at the pictures and listen.

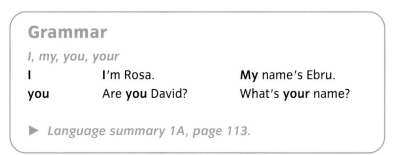

Grammar

I, my, you, your

I	I'm Rosa.	**My** name's Ebru.
you	Are **you** David?	What's **your** name?

▶ *Language summary 1A, page 113.*

Pronunciation

1 ▭ [1.2] Listen and practise.

I'm a student.
What's your name?
My name's Ebru.
Nice to meet you.

2 Complete the conversations with *I, my, you,* or *your.*

a) What's ...your.. name, please? — Abdul Hussein.

b) Hi, ...'m Martina. What's .... name? — .... name's Vanessa.

c) Hello, are .... Mr Bellini? — Yes, that's right.

d) Hello, ... name's Peter Gregory. — Hi, ...'m Andrea Martin. Nice to meet you.

e) Are .... Mrs Adams? — No, ...'m Mrs Davis.

3 **a)** [1.3] Listen and check.

b) Repeat the conversations. Practise with a partner.

Speaking task

1 Practise saying your name in English.

2 Introduce yourself to other students in the class.

Hi, my name's Petra.

Hello, I'm Sunan.

Focus 2

Vocabulary: jobs; a/an

1 Match the jobs with the pictures a–h.

> teacher   student
> waiter   doctor   actor
> police officer   engineer
> businessman/businesswoman
>
> ▶ Vocabulary book page 3.

Example: picture b – actor

Pronunciation

1 ▭ [1.4] Listen to the jobs. Notice the stress.
tėacher   studėnt

2 Listen again and repeat.

2 ▭ [1.5] Listen. Who is speaking?

Example: 1 – doctor

3 ▭ [1.6] Listen and complete.

a) I'm ..a waiter.. .   c) I'm ....

b) I'm ....   d) I'm ....

Grammar

Jobs + a/an

a + consonant (b, c, d, ...)   an + vowel (a, e, i, o, u)
I'm **a** doctor.   I'm **an** actor.

▶ *Language summary 1B, page 113.*

4 Write the jobs in Exercise 1 in the correct place.

a student

(a)   (an)

5 What's your job? Ask and answer with other students.

(What's your job?)   (I'm a ...)

he/she/his/her

6 ▭ [1.7] Match the sentences with the pictures. Listen and check.

▶ Vocabulary book page 3.

1 His name's Tony Blair. He's a politician.
picture b

2 Her name's Serena Williams. She's a tennis player.

3 His name's Luis Figo. He's a footballer.

4 Her name's Jennifer Lopez. She's a singer and an actress.

Grammar

He/she/his/her

She's a singer. **Her** name's Jennifer Lopez.
He's a footballer. **His** name's Luis Figo.

▶ *Language summary 1A, page 113.*

7 **a)** ▭ [1.8] Listen to the questions and answers. Listen again and repeat.

What's his name?   What's his job?

What's her name?   What's her job?

b) Point to the pictures. Ask and answer in pairs.

Reading

8 Match A and B.

A	B
full name	Tony
first name	Blair
surname	Anthony Charles Lynton Blair

9 Complete the questions with *his* or *her*.

a What's ..his.. full name?

Tom Cruise

b What's .... first name?

President Putin

c What's .... surname?

Madonna

d What's .... full name?

Tiger Woods

10 Match questions a–d with answers 1–4.

1 [b] His first name is Vladimir. His full name is Vladimir Vladimirovich Putin.

2 [ ] Her surname is Ciccone. Her full name is Madonna Louise Veronica Ciccone.

3 [ ] His full name is Thomas Cruise Mapother IV.

4 [ ] His first name is not really Tiger. His full name is Eldrick Woods.

Focus 3

The alphabet; *How do you spell ...?*

1 🔲 [1.9] Listen and say the alphabet.

2 🔲 [1.10] Listen and say the missing letters.

3 Say these:

EMI

IBM.®

BBC

KLM uk

DKNY

BMW

4 **a)** 🔲 [1.11] Listen and answer the questions you hear.

b) Choose five more English words. Ask your partner the spelling.

How do you spell 'hello'?

h-e-l-l-o

Speaking task

1 🔲 [1.12] Listen and complete the questions.

a) What's your .... ?
b) And .... your first name?
c) What's your .... , please?
d) And .... do you .... that, please?

2 Ask the full names of four students in your class. Complete the gaps below.

Full name: _____

Full name: _____

First name: _____

Surname: _____

First name: _____

Surname: _____

Real life

hello and *goodbye*

1 🔊 [1.13] Listen and put the conversations in order.

a)
☐	– Hi, Antonia. Nice to meet you.
1	– Paula, this is Antonia.
☐	– Nice to meet you!

c)
☐	– Yes, see you!
☐	– Goodbye!
☐	– Bye, Kris. See you later.

2 Listen again and repeat.

3 Practise the conversations with other students. Use **your** names.

Goodbye!

Bye, Ali. See you later.

b)
☐	– Fine, thank you. And you?
☐	– Hello, Steve!
☐	– Hello, how are you?
☐	– I'm very well, thanks.

Focus 4

Numbers 0–20

1   [1.14] Listen and say the numbers.
▶ Vocabulary book page 4.

2   Write a number. Your partner says it.

3   **a)** Match the words with the numbers.

eighteen	fifteen	fourteen
nineteen	seventeen	
sixteen	thirteen	twenty

b)   [1.15] Listen and check. Say the words.

4   Turn to pages 108, 110 and 112, and play bingo!

Real life

Classroom language

5 Point to these things in your classroom.

> a student   a pen   your teacher   your book
> a picture in your book   page 6 in your book

6 Match the phrases to the pictures.

> listen   say your name   write your name
> open your book a   close your book
> look   read your book   work in pairs
>
> ▶ Vocabulary book page 5.

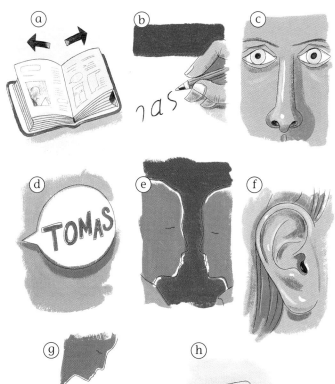

7 🔊 [1.16] Listen and follow the instructions.

8 Work in pairs. Give **five** instructions to your partner. Your partner does what you say.

▶ Language summary, page 113
▶ Vocabulary book, pages 2–6

1 Put the words in the correct order.

a) full/your/name/What's ?
   What's your full name?

b) you/are/How ?

c) job/his/What's ?

d) How/spell/do/'Antonia'/you ?

e) surname/her/What's ?

2 Complete the job words 1–10 and find the extra job!

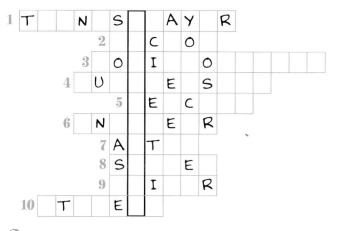

3 Write the answers. You have two minutes!

a) one + seven – three = *five*

b) three + four + six =

c) twenty – seventeen + nine =

d) four + eight – five =

e) fifteen – nine – two =

f) nineteen – eleven + four =

4 Put these words in the gaps. Then practise the conversation.

> Nice   ~~Hello~~   Hi   thanks   How
> meet   well   fine   this

STEFAN: a) ..*Hello*.. , Marta.

MARTA: b) .... , Stefan! c) .... are you?

STEFAN: I'm d) .... , e) .... And you?

MARTA: I'm very f) .... , thanks.

STEFAN: Marta, g) .... is Annette.

ANNETTE: Hello, Marta. h) .... to meet you.

MARTA: Nice to i) .... you.

Around the world

▶ **Grammar:** *be* with *I, you, he, she* and *it*
▶ **Vocabulary:** countries and nationalities; numbers 21–100; *How old ...?*
▶ **Real life:** phone numbers; filling in a form

Focus 1

Vocabulary: countries

1 **a)** Match the country with the number.

> Great Britain   Brazil   Poland
> France   Italy   Russia
> Spain   Japan   Turkey
> the USA
>
> ▶ Vocabulary Book page 7.

Example: 1 - the USA

b) 🖭 [2.1] Listen and check.

> **Pronunciation**
>
> 🖭 [2.2] Listen and repeat.
>
> Brazil   Turkey   Italy

2 Say a number. Your partner says the country.

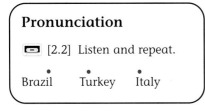

What's number 1?

The USA.

be with *I* and *you*

3 Where are you from? Say your country in English. Ask other students.

Where are you from?   *I'm from France.*

> **Grammar**
>
> *be* with *I* and *you*
>
> question: Where **are you** from?   **Are you** from Italy?
>
> answer: **I'm** from France.
>   (= **I am**)
>
> ▶ *Language summary 2, page 113.*

Listening

4 📼 [2.3] Listen to the conversation. Where are the people from?

5 **a)** Put the conversation in order.

a) ☐ 1 Where are you from?
b) ☐ Are you a student?
c) ☐ I'm from Russia.
d) ☐ 2 I'm from São Paulo, in Brazil. And you?
e) ☐ No, I'm not from Moscow, I'm from St Petersburg.
f) ☐ Are you from Moscow?
g) ☐ 7 Yes, I'm at St Petersburg University.

b) Listen and check. Practise the conversation.

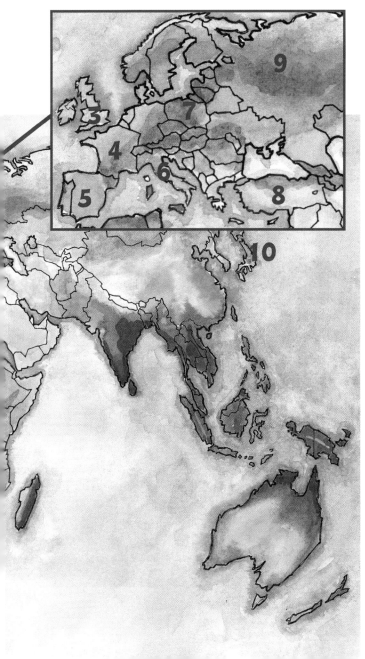

6 Write a conversation. Practise with a partner.

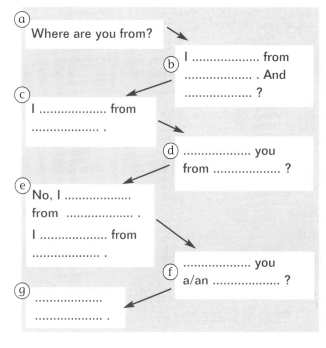

ⓐ Where are you from?

ⓑ I .... from .... And .... ?

ⓒ I .... from ....

ⓓ .... you from .... ?

ⓔ No, I .... from .... I .... from ....

ⓕ .... you a/an .... ?

ⓖ ....

Grammar

be: negative

I	I'm **not** from Moscow. (= **am not**)
you	You **aren't** from Great Britain. (= **are not**)

▶ *Language summary 2, page 113.*

---

7 **a)** Are these sentences true (T) or false (F) for you?

a) ☐ I'm from Great Britain.
b) ☐ I'm from a small country.
c) ☐ I'm a doctor.
d) ☐ I'm from a big city.
e) ☐ I'm a student.
f) ☐ I'm from the capital city of my country.
g) ☐ I'm from New York.
h) ☐ I'm an English teacher.

b) Correct the wrong sentences.

Example: I'm not from Great Britain, I'm from Poland.

Focus 2

Nationalities; *be* with *he*, *she* and *it*

1 Match the country with the nationality.
▶ Vocabulary book page 8.

Country	Nationality
Great Britain	French
France	American
the USA	Japanese
Japan	British
Italy	Russian
Russia	Italian

2 Do the quiz.

3 ▭ [2.4] Listen and check your answers.

Grammar

be: he/she/it

⊕
He**'s** American. (= **is**)
She**'s** a tennis player.
It**'s** in Istanbul.

⊖
He **isn't** Italian. (= **is not**)
She **isn't** a singer.
It **isn't** in Cairo.

▶ *Language summary 2, page 113.*

4 Write *is*/**'s** or *isn't* in the spaces.

a) Leonardo DiCaprio .... Italian, he .... American.

b) The Blue Mosque .... in Istanbul. It .... in Cairo.

c) Anna Kournikova .... a singer, she .... a tennis player.

Quiz

1) The Blue Mosque's in:
a) Cairo.
b) Istanbul.
c) Baghdad.

2) Leonardo DiCaprio is:
a) British.
b) Italian.
c) American.

3) Anna Kournikova is:
a) a singer.
b) an actress.
c) a tennis player.

4) Rivaldo is from:
a) Brazil. ✓
b) Italy.
c) Spain.

5) Sony is:
a) a Japanese company.
b) a British company.
c) an American company.

6) A Ferrari is:
a) an American car.
b) a Spanish car.
c) an Italian car.

5 Correct the sentences.

a) Microsoft is a British company.

Microsoft isn't a British company. It's an American company.

b) Tony Blair is an actor.

c) A Rolls Royce is an Italian car.

d) Rio de Janeiro is in Spain.

e) Martina Hingis is an actress.

f) Buckingham Palace is in New York.

g) Vladimir Putin is the President of the USA.

h) Fiat is a Spanish company.

i) Hillary Clinton is French.

Pronunciation

1 🔊 [2.5] Listen and practise.

He's …	**He's** a politician.
She's …	**She's** British.
It's …	**It's** in London.
… isn't …	He **isn't** an actor.
	She **isn't** French.

---

6 a) Write six sentences, three true and three false.

Sydney is in Australia.
Nintendo is a French company.

b) Say the sentences to your partner.

Nintendo is a French company.

False. It's a Japanese company.

Questions

7 a) Look at the pictures and match the people with the countries.

Germany   Italy   Australia   Egypt   Spain   Thailand

b) 🔊 [2.6] Ask and answer. Listen and check.

Where's Claudia from?

She's from Italy.

Grammar

he and *she* questions

Where**'s he** from?   **He's** from Australia.
Where**'s she** from?   **She's** from Thailand.

▶ *Language summary 2, page 113.*

8 Ask about the other students in your class.

Focus 3

Numbers 21–100

1 ▢ [2.7] Say the numbers.

20 twenty **30** thirty **40** forty

50 fifty **60** sixty

70 seventy **80** eighty **90** ninety

100 a hundred

2 **a)** Write the missing numbers.
▶ Vocabulary book page 9.

20 twenty	25 ....
21 twenty-one	26 ....
22 twenty-two	27 ....
23 *twenty-three*	28 ....
24	29 twenty-nine

b) ▢ [2.8] Listen and check.
Practise saying the numbers.

c) Say these numbers.

32 45 58 63 77 89 91

3 ▢ [2.9] Listen and write the numbers you hear.

4 Say a number. Your partner says the next three numbers.

fifty-eight

fifty-nine, sixty, sixty-one

b

a

c

Ages

5 How old are the people in the photos?

How old is she?

I don't know.

I think she's about twenty-two.

she's fifty-nine	he's forty-eight	she's fifteen
he's twenty-two	she's thirty-eight	he's two
he's forty-seven	she's fifty-five	he's six
he's ninety-two	she's twenty	she's thirty-three

6 ■ [2.10] Listen and check.

7 How old are you?

> I'm fifteen.

> I'm thirty-four.

1 ■ [2.11] Look at two photos of a teacher's friends. Listen and complete the information.

Nikos ....

Athens in Greece

Job?

a) ....

How old?

b) ....

Name?

c) ....

Where from?

d) ....

teacher

28

2 Work in pairs.
Either:
Show your partner two or three photos of your friends. Your partner asks questions.
Or:
Your partner thinks of two friends. Ask questions and complete the table.

	Friend A	Friend B
Name?		
Where from?		
Job?		
How old?		

Real life

Phone numbers

1 **a)** How do you say these phone numbers?

a) 020 8567 0322

b) 01902 235996

c) 00 34 16 835 1267

b) 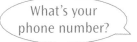 [2.12] Listen and check.

2 Ask five students for their phone numbers.

What's your phone number?

It's 0956 421388.

Listening

3 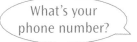 [2.13] Listen and find four mistakes on the form.

4 Complete the questions with **are** or **'s**.

a) What ..'s.... your surname?

b) What .... your first name?

c) .... you married?

d) How old .... you?

e) What .... your address?

f) What .... your phone number?

g) What .... your job?

First name:	Single:	Married:
Rita		✔

Surname:	Job:
Kirmala	teacher

Age:

30

Address:

87 Stanley Road
London
SE6 1BH

Phone number home:

020 8695 2441

work:

020 7233 8424

Send form   Clear form

Pronunciation

1 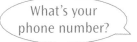 [2.14] Listen to the questions in Exercise 4. Notice the stress.

What's your surname?

2 Listen and repeat.

Speaking task

Filling in a form

Interview another student and complete the form.

Don't forget!

"My surname's Jones."

"How do you spell that?"

First name ....

Surname ....

Single ☐   Married ☐

Age ....

Address ....

....

Phone number: home ....

work ....

Job ....

Do you remember?

▶ Language summary, page 113
▶ Vocabulary book, pages 7–11

1 *is/'s* or *are*?

a) Where *'s/are* you from?

b) What *'s/are* his job?

c) How old *is/are* you?

d) *Is/Are* she a doctor?

e) Where *'s/are* the White House?

2 Match 1–5 with a–e in Exercise 1.

1) I'm forty-six.

2) It's in Washington.

3) I'm from Sydney, in Australia. a

4) No, she's a teacher.

5) He's a businessman.

3 Write the next two numbers.

a) a hundred, eighty, sixty ...forty, twenty...

b) seventy-four, sixty-eight, sixty-two ....

c) twelve, twenty-four, thirty-six ....

d) seventeen, twenty-six, thirty-five ....

4 Find **ten** countries. You have three minutes!

W	G	R	E	A	T	B	R	I	T	A	I	N	S
J	S	R	A	M	N	O	D	E	V	I	L	E	E
V	R	E	P	O	Y	N	N	A	F	T	A	R	S
P	B	G	E	R	M	A	N	Y	B	A	K	U	R
O	M	Y	S	S	O	T	F	Q	O	L	C	S	A
L	S	P	K	C	U	F	R	A	N	Y	I	S	T
A	I	T	H	A	I	L	A	N	D	M	R	I	Y
N	J	M	R	E	P	S	N	A	W	S	P	A	M
D	B	J	A	P	A	N	C	R	S	P	A	I	N
O	F	A	W	I	R	P	E	G	T	A	W	T	C
Q	B	O	N	L	L	A	M	S	S	K	R	A	M

5 Choose the correct word or phrase.

a) I'm from Rio de Janeiro, a *city/company* in Brazil.

b) A Renault is a French *car/address*.

c) Madrid is the *city/capital city* of Spain.

d) Coca-Cola is an American *company/surname*.

e) My *first name/address* is 22 Argyle Street, Manchester.

f) Her *company/phone number* is 01902 432776.

module 3
In a different country

▶ **Grammar:** *be:* plural; plural nouns; *this/that/these/those*
▶ **Vocabulary:** places; food and drink; common adjectives
▶ **Real life:** in a café; prices

Focus 1

Vocabulary: places; plural nouns

1 Look at the pictures. Which countries are they?

Example: a – the USA, I think.

2 Find these things in the pictures.

> a man   a bus   a house   a woman
> a taxi   a child   a shop   a car
>
> ▶ Vocabulary book page 12.

3 Answer the questions. You have two minutes!

1 How many taxis are there in picture b? two
2 How many shops are there in picture e?
3 How many buses are there in picture d?
4 How many houses are there in picture a?
5 How many people are there in picture c?

Grammar

Singular nouns	Plural nouns
a taxi + **s**	two taxi**s**
a car + **s**	twenty car**s**
Look!	
a bus + **es**	four bus**es**
a city → **ies**	two cit**ies**
Irregular nouns	
a **man**	two **men**
a **woman**	three **women**
a **child**	five **children**
a **person**	fifty **people**

▶ *Language summary 3B, page 114.*

be: plural

5 Find **three** false sentences.

a) The Pyramids are in Turkey. *false*

b) New York taxis are yellow.

c) The Eiffel Tower is in Rome.

d) London buses are red.

e) The Hilton is an expensive hotel.

f) New York and London are capital cities.

Grammar

be: plural form

The Pyramids **are** in Egypt.

London buses **are** red.

Washington and London **are** capital cities.

▶ *Language summary 3A, page 114.*

---

6 a) Make true sentences from boxes a, b and c.

Paris and Madrid are capital cities.

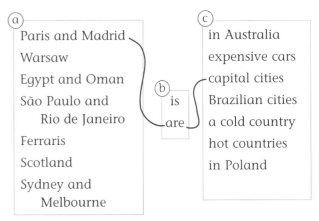

ⓐ
Paris and Madrid
Warsaw
Egypt and Oman
São Paulo and
    Rio de Janeiro
Ferraris
Scotland
Sydney and
    Melbourne

ⓑ
is
are

ⓒ
in Australia
expensive cars
capital cities
Brazilian cities
a cold country
hot countries
in Poland

b) 🔲 [3.2] Listen and check.

7 Write two true sentences and two false sentences. Say them to your partner.

Tokyo and Beijing are capital cities.

True.

England's a hot country.

False!

Pronunciation

1 🔲 [3.1] Listen and practise the singular and plural nouns.

4 Write the plurals.

a) shop – *shops*

b) country

c) actress

d) businesswoman

e) teacher

f) businessman

g) house

h) company

i) address

Focus 2

Reading and vocabulary

1 Look at the pictures and read about the people.

a) Where are they from?

b) Where are they now?

c) Who is – on holiday?

– at a language school?

2 Check the words in the box and read the email and the postcard. Complete the table. ▶ Vocabulary book page 13.

☺☺ = fantastic, very good   ☹ = not very good
☺ = good/nice   ☹☹ = awful!

	Helen, Stewart and Amy	Renata and Claudia
rooms	☺	
food		
weather		
other people		

3 Are Helen, Stewart and Amy happy in Alicante? Are Renata and Claudia happy in Oxford?

Helen, Stewart and Amy are from Scotland. They are on holiday in Spain.

Hi!

We're here in Spain, in Alicante! The weather is fantastic and we're really happy with our hotel. Our rooms are nice, and the food is very good. Only one problem – the other Scottish people in the hotel are awful!

See you soon,
Love Helen, Stewart and Amy
XXXXX

David and Kathleen Spencer,
14, Burlington Avenue,
Edinburgh,
Scotland
UK

Renata and Claudia are from Brazil. They are language students at the Europa School in Oxford.

Message

From: Renata
To: Rachel and Max
Sent: Renata and Claudia
Subject: Hello

Hi Rachel and Max,

How are you? We're here - IN ENGLAND!!! We're at the Europa School in Oxford. The school's fantastic - the teachers are very good and the other students are nice. They're from all over the world - Japan, Poland, Russia, Italy ... everywhere! We're really happy here, but we aren't very happy with our rooms - they're expensive and they aren't very big. The weather's good, but the food is AWFUL!!! See you soon!

Love Renata and Claudia XXXXXXXXX

be with *we* and *they*

4 Read Renata and Claudia's email again. Circle the correct verb form to make true sentences.

a) Our school *is*/*isn't* very good.

b) The food *is*/*isn't* very nice.

c) The other students *are*/*aren't* very nice.

d) Our rooms *are*/*aren't* very big.

e) We *are*/*aren't* very happy here.

f) We *are*/*aren't* very happy with our rooms.

Grammar

be with *we* and *they*

We	➕	We're very happy here. (= we are)
	➖	We **aren't** very happy here. (= are not)
They	➕	They're expensive. (= they are)
	➖	They **aren't** very big.

▶ *Language summary 3A, page 114.*

Pronunciation

1 🔲 [3.3] Listen and tick (✓) the sentences you hear.

1a) We're from Brazil.   b)   They're from Brazil.

2a) They aren't students. b)   We aren't students.

3a) They're married.   b)   They aren't married.

4a) We're on holiday.   b)   We aren't on holiday.

2 Listen again and repeat.

---

5 a) Look at the pictures and read the sentences. Complete the sentences with *is*/*isn't* or *are*/*aren't*.

b) 🔲 [3.4] Listen and check your answers.

6 a) Write three sentences about a group of people on pages 24 and 25. Don't write their names.

They're from Scotland.
They're in Spain. They're on holiday.

b) Work in pairs. Read your sentences to your partner. Your partner says who they are.

People in London

"We .`'re`..... from Beirut in Lebanon, and we .... in London on holiday. We .... staying with friends from Lebanon, and we .... very happy here. London .... beautiful, but the weather .... very good!"

The Karam family

"I'm from Milan, and Emre .... from Ankara in Turkey. We .... on holiday, we .... students at London University. London .... fantastic for students, but it .... very expensive!"

Bruno and Emre

"We .... from St Petersburg in Russia. We .... doctors, and we .... in London for a conference. The conference .... very good, but we .... very happy with our hotel. It .... very expensive and the rooms .... very small."

Irina and Ivan

Focus 3

Vocabulary: food and drink

1 Match these words with the pictures in the quiz.

> bread   meat   rice
> coffee   pasta   fish   fruit
> milk   water   eggs
> vegetables   cheese
>
> ▶ Vocabulary book page 14.

bread – picture d

2 Put the words into these groups.

food	drink
bread	

3 🔊 [3.5] Listen and check. Practise saying the words.

4 a) Complete the quiz.

b) Compare answers with other students.

> I like coffee, cheese, and …

> My favourite drink is water!

> I don't like fruit.

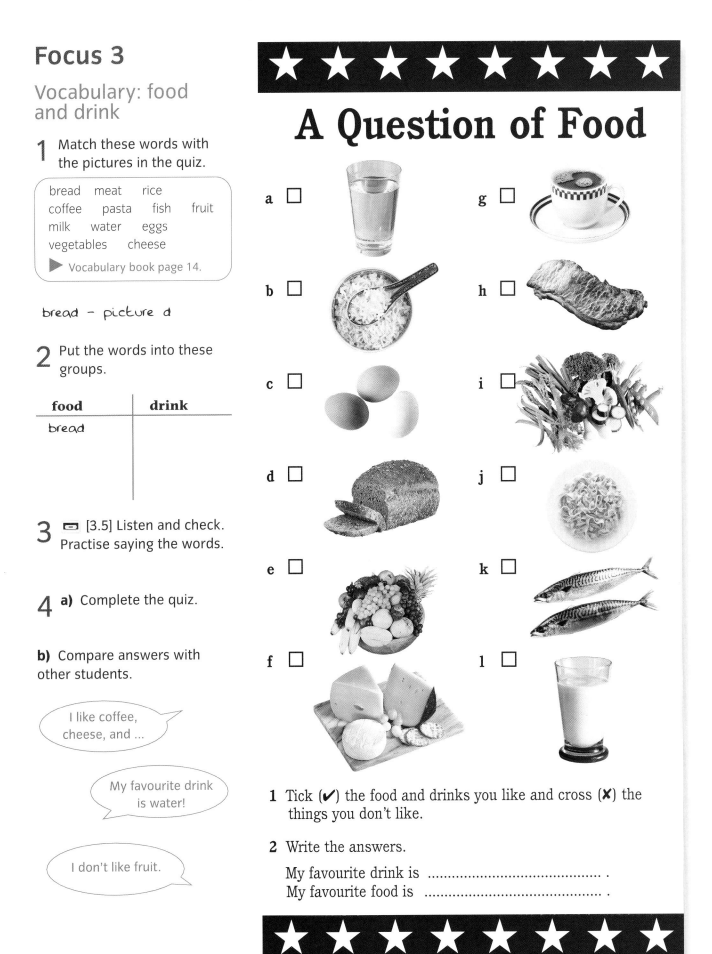

A Question of Food

a ☐   g ☐

b ☐   h ☐

c ☐   i ☐

d ☐   j ☐

e ☐   k ☐

f ☐   l ☐

1 Tick (✔) the food and drinks you like and cross (✗) the things you don't like.

2 Write the answers.

My favourite drink is ....
My favourite food is ....

(a) Dad, what's *this/that*?

It's cheese, Sam.

(b) Look at *this/that* old car!

Yes, it's beautiful.

(c) Are *those/these* bananas?

Yes, they're red bananas.

(d) *These/Those* shoes are nice.

Yes, they are.

this, that, these, those

5 🔊 [3.6] Listen and (circle) the correct word in conversations a–d. Practise the conversations.

Grammar

this, that, these, those

singular	↓ *this* cheese	↘ *that* car
	What's *this*?	What's *that*?
plural	↓ *these* bananas	↘ *those* shoes
	What are *these*?	What are *those*?

▶ *Language summary 3C, page 114.*

6 a) Complete the sentences with *this, that, these* or *those*.

(a) Look! What's .... building?

(b) Who are .... children?

(c) .... postcards, please.

(d) Tomas, ... is Vanessa. Vanessa, ... is Tomas.

b) 🔊 [3.7] Listen and check.

Real life

In a café; prices

1 a) 🔲 [3.8] Number the prices in the order you hear them.

☐	€4.00	☐	6.25
☐ I	$12.50	☐	59.99
☐	£3.70	☐	7.90
☐	45p		

b) Practise saying the prices.

2 a) Find these in the pictures.

> a sandwich   chips   a bottle of coke
> a burger   a salad   a pizza
>
> ▶ Vocabulary book page 15.

b) 🔲 [3.9] Listen and repeat.

3 a) Look at the pictures above. Write these phrases in conversations a, b or c.

> How much is that?   No, thanks.
> Thank you.   Three coffees, please.
> ~~A burger and chips, please.~~

b) 🔲 [3.10] Listen and check. Practise the conversations with a partner.

4 Practise conversations a, b and c again with these words.

a

a pizza and a burger

two cheese sandwiches

an egg sandwich and a salad

b

two cokes

a coffee with milk

a bottle of water

c

3.20   8.60   6.95

Example:

28

Five ninety, please.

Listening

5 🔊 [3.11] Listen to a conversation in a café. Tick (✔) what the customers order.

food		drinks	
cheese sandwich	☐	**coke**	☐
egg sandwich	☐	**coffee**	☐
pizza	☐	**bottle of water**	☐
burger	☐		
chips	☐		
salad	☐		

Speaking task

1 Look at the menu on page 112. Work in groups and write a conversation in a café.

2 Learn your conversation and act it for the class.

Do you remember?

▶ Language summary, page 114
▶ Vocabulary book, pages 12–16

1 Choose the correct answer.

a) *(That)/This* 's my new car over there.

b) Is *this/these* my Vocabulary Book?

c) *That/Those* people are teachers from Italy.

d) *This/These* city is very beautiful.

e) Are *that/those* your children?

f) *This/These* is my address in the USA.

2 Write the plurals.

a) bottle ...bottles...........   e) sandwich ....

b) vegetable ....   f) country ....

c) address ....   g) house ....

d) child ....   h) woman ....

3 What are these adjectives? You have two minutes!

a) D C L O cold..............   f) C E N I n...............

b) T H O h......................   g) O D G O g.............

c) L U W F A a...............   h) I G B b.................

d) X E N I E V P E S e...

e) C A N S T I T A F f...

4 Write the words in the correct place.

a man	~~a bus~~	a house	a woman	a taxi
a hotel	a child	a shop	a car	

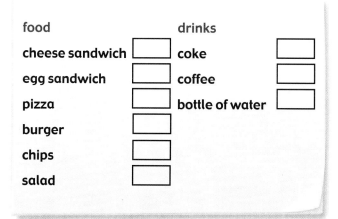

PEOPLE

BUILDINGS

TRANSPORT

a bus

module 4

Around town

- ▶ **Grammar:** *there is/there are; a, some* and *any*
- ▶ **Vocabulary:** places in a town; prepositions; common adjectives
- ▶ **Real life:** in the street

Focus 1

Vocabulary: places in a town

1 Which places can you see in the pictures?

a bank   a park   a hotel
a post office   a bus stop
a cinema   a supermarket
a restaurant   a car park
a station   a café   a square

▶ Vocabulary book page 17.

2 Look at the town map on page 31. Which places are numbers 1–11?

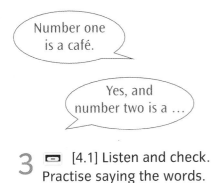

Number one is a café.

Yes, and number two is a …

3 ▭ [4.1] Listen and check. Practise saying the words.

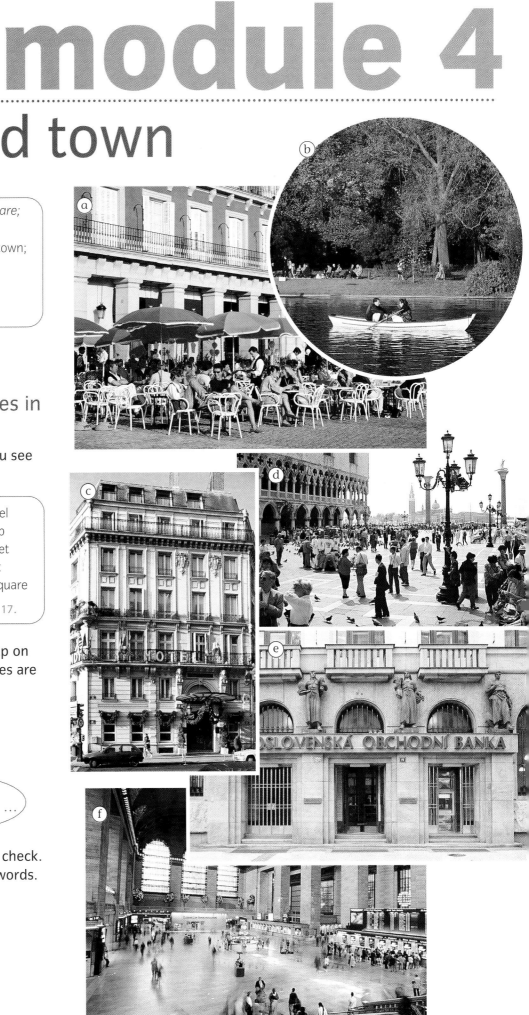

SLOVENSKÁ OBCHODNÍ BANKA

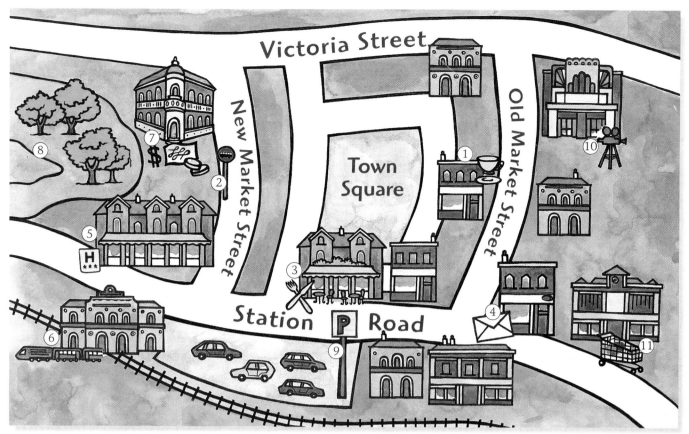

Prepositions

4 a) Match the prepositions with the diagrams.

on the left   on the right
in   near

▶ Vocabulary book page 18.

① ② ③ ④

b) Look at the map. Are the sentences true (T) or false (F)?

a) The station's in the square.

b) The station's on the left of the car park.

c) The restaurant's on the right of the post office.

d) The bus stop's near the hotel.

5 Circle the correct answer.

a) The bus stop's near the (bank)/station.

b) The car park's in Station Road/Victoria Street.

c) The car park's on the right/on the left of the station.

d) The supermarket's on the left/on the right of the post office.

e) The bank's in Old Market Street/New Market Street.

f) The bank/cinema 's near the park.

g) The hotel's near the restaurant/cinema.

h) The bus stop is/isn't in the square.

6 Make sentences about these places.

a) cinema – Old Market Street.
   The cinema is in Old Market Street.

b) café – square

c) post office – supermarket

d) park – bank

e) cinema – café

f) post office – Station Road

g) hotel – park

7 Work in pairs. You are in the car park. Ask and answer questions.

Excuse me, where's the supermarket?

It's over there, near the post office.

31

Focus 2

Listening

1 Look at the picture. Find:

> a tree   a boy   a girl
> a baby   a dog
>
> ▶ Vocabulary book page 18.

2 ▭ [4.2] Listen to two descriptions. Which is correct – A or B?

there is, there are

3 Tick (✓) the true sentences.

a) [✗] In the café, there's a woman with her baby.

b) [✓] There are three or four young women in the café.

c) [ ] There are two waiters in the café.

d) [ ] On the left of the café, there's a hotel.

e) [ ] On the right of the café, there's a restaurant.

f) [ ] There are two girls and two boys in the square.

g) [ ] There are two dogs in the square.

h) [ ] There are a lot of trees in the square.

i) [ ] There are two old women near the tree.

Grammar

There is and *there are*

Singular
There's a hotel.
(= **there is**)

Plural
There are two dogs.

▶ *Language summary 4A,*
  page 114.

4 Correct the wrong
  sentences in Exercise 3.

There's one waiter in the café.

5 Write four more sentences
  about the picture.

There's a dog near the café.

There's a tree in the square.

Pronunciation

1 ▭ [4.3] Listen. Practise saying 'th'.

/ð/   there   they   the
this   that   these   those

2 ▭ [4.4] This is the other 'th' sound. Listen and practise.

/θ/   three   thirteen
thirty   think   thing

Speaking task

1 a) Work in groups.
Group A: look at picture A below.
Group B: look at picture B
on page 111.

b) Make sentences to describe
your picture.

2 a) Work in pairs. Find **eight**
differences between picture A
and B.

b) Tell the class about the
differences.

Don't forget!

"In my picture there's a
(*café*)."

"Yes, in my picture too."

"There are two (*cars*) in
my picture."

"There's a (*big tree*) on the
right of the (*café*)."

Picture A

Focus 3

Reading and vocabulary

1 Look at the three texts quickly. Where are the people from?

2 Which Kingston is:

a) a city? Jamaica.   d) near a river?

b) a large town?   e) near the sea?

c) a small town?   f) near a lake?

3 **a)** Check the words and phrases in **bold** below.

▶ Vocabulary book page 17.

Kingston, Jamaica	1 There's a lot of reggae **music**. 2 There are some **beautiful beaches**. 3 It's **near London**.
Kingston, England	4 There's a **famous train**. 5 It's very **busy**. 6 There are some **beautiful** parks.
Kingston, New Zealand	7 It's very **quiet**. 8 It's **not beautiful**, but it's **interesting**. 9 It's in the **mountains**.

b) 🔊 [4.5] Listen and read the texts. Which three sentences are in the wrong place?

a, some and *any*

4 Look at the three Kingston texts again. Which place do you **think** these sentences describe?

a) There isn't a university.

b) There aren't any mountains.

c) There are some big hotels.

My home town Kingston

Gloria Seaga is a teacher from Kingston, Jamaica.

Kingston, Jamaica (population 700,000)

"Kingston isn't a beautiful city, but it's very busy and interesting. There are lots of people, lots of cafés, and there's reggae music everywhere! There are some beautiful places near Kingston – the Blue Mountains – and some beautiful beaches. It's a fantastic place!"

Grammar

a, some and *any*

Singular ➕ There's **a** famous train.

       ➖ There isn't **a** university.

       ❓ Is there **a** river?

Plural ➕ There are **some** parks.

       ➖ There aren't **any** mountains.

       ❓ Are there **any** beaches?

▶ *Language summary 4B, page 114.*

5 Think of a town – **not** your town! Write five sentences about these things.

mountains	a river	a lake	big shops
beautiful parks		a university	a beach

There are some mountains near ...

There isn't a university in ...

Nikita Aziz is a student at the University of Kingston, near London.

Kingston-upon-Thames, England (population 150,000)

"Kingston's a very busy town. There are a lot of shops and cars, and there's a university with students from all over the world! But it's a nice place – there's an old market square, and we're near the River Thames. There are some beautiful parks too."

Gavin Watt is a taxi driver from Kingston, New Zealand.

Kingston, New Zealand (population 2,000)

"Kingston's a small town near Lake Wakatipu in the mountains. It's in a really beautiful place, but it's very quiet – there's only one school, one bank and one small supermarket! There's a famous old train here too, and some restaurants for the tourists."

Speaking task

1 Write **ten** questions to ask another student about where he/she lives.

Are there any good restaurants near your house?

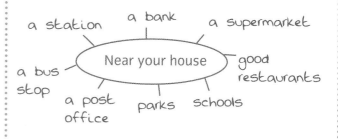

a station   a bank   a supermarket

a bus stop — Near your house — good restaurants

a post office   parks   schools

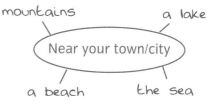

mountains   a lake

Near your town/city

a beach   the sea

2 Interview another student.

Don't forget!

"There are five (*supermarkets*)."

"No there isn't a (*station*), but there's a (*bus stop*)."

"Yes, it's near the sea – and there's a (*beautiful beach*) too."

Writing

3 Write a paragraph about where you live.

In Latina there are some good restaurants and there's a beautiful park. There's a famous university, but there aren't any beaches. Near my house ...

Real life

In the street

1 Match the sentences with the pictures.

> Excuse me, where's the station? That's okay.
> Sorry, I don't understand. ~~Sorry, I don't know.~~

2 🔲 [4.6] Listen and check.

> **Pronunciation**
>
> 1 🔲 [4.7] Listen.
>
> Sorry.   That's okay.
>
> Sorry, I don't know.
>
> Sorry, I don't understand.
>
> Excuse me, where's the station?
>
> 2 Listen again and repeat.

3 Work in pairs. Practise the conversations.

4 Imagine you are in the street. Make different conversations with other students.

Excuse me, where's the post office?

It's over there.

Do you remember?

▶ Language summary, page 114
▶ Vocabulary book, pages 17–21

1 Circle the correct answer.
a) *There's*/*There are* a bus stop near the bank.
b) *Is there*/*Are there* any people in the park?
c) There are *some*/*any* nice restaurants in the square.
d) There isn't *a*/*any* university in this town.
e) There aren't *some*/*any* mountains near this city.
f) *There's*/*There are* a supermarket near the station.

2 Are these sentences true (T) or false (F) for you? Correct the false sentences.
a) There are fifteen students in our class. F
  There are twenty-one students in this class.
b) There's a park near our school.
c) There are some pictures in this classroom.
d) There's a café in our school.
e) There are twenty chairs in this classroom.
f) There's a cinema near our school.
g) There aren't any women in this class.

3 Put the word in the correct place.
a) There's a bank ^near the station. (*near*)
b) London's very interesting city. (*a*)
c) There's a post office the left of the bank. (*on*)
d) Excuse me, are there cafés in this street? (*any*)
e) In Paris there are very good restaurants. (*some*)
f) The cinema is on the right the supermarket. (*of*)
g) We're in a café Baker Street. (*in*)

4 Write the vowels in these adjectives. Write two things for each adjective.
a) S M a L L   a small café   a small school
b) _ N T _ R _ S T _ N G   e) B _ SY
c) Q _ _ _ T   f) F _ M _ _ S
d) N _ C _   g) B _ _ _ T _ F _ L

5 Complete the crossword with places in a town. You have four minutes!

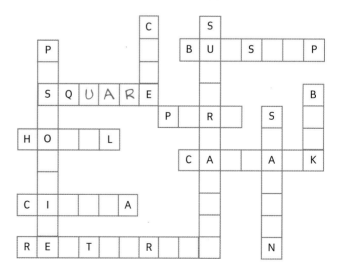

Consolidation ── modules 1-4

A Grammar and reading: the verb *be*

Write a part of *be* in the gaps. Use contractions ('s, 're, isn't, etc.) where possible.

Dear Matt,

Hi, from Australia! Janie and I
(a) *are* now in Melbourne. We
(b) .... with two old friends
from university, Rick and Tanya,
and it (c) .... good to see them
again.
Melbourne is a really nice city. It
(d – negative) .... very big, and
the people (e) .... very friendly.
There (f) .... some beautiful
parks and lots of shops and
cinemas, but there
(g – negative) .... any
interesting markets.
Melbourne's famous in Australia
for its food, and there (h) ....
lots of different types of
restaurants here — Chinese,
Italian, Vietnamese, Thai — and
the food (i – negative) ....
expensive. The weather (j) ....
beautiful and I (k) .... very
happy here!

See you soon.
Steve

B Grammar and speaking: questions with *you*

1 Put the questions in order.

a) name/'s/What/your ?
   What's your name?
b) from/you/are/Where ?
c) job/your/'s/What ?
d) you/How/are/old ?
e) Are/married/you ?
f) your/What/address/'s ?
g) 's/What/number/phone/your ?
h) a university/there/Is/in your city ?

2 ▭ [1] Match the questions in Exercise 1 with these answers. Listen and check.

1) I'm an engineer.
2) Avenida San Martin No 9-159.
3) No, I'm single.
4) 575 665 7433
5) Julia Maria Campos. *a*
6) Yes, there is.
7) I'm thirty-six.
8) I'm from Cartajena, in Colombia.

3 Work with a student you don't know. Ask and answer the questions in Exercise 1.

C Vocabulary: odd one out

1 Which word is different? Why?

a) bread, meat, milk
b) France, Poland, Spanish
c) a school, a doctor, a teacher
d) a cinema, a town, a car park
e) a boy, a tree, a girl
f) coffee, cheese, water
g) a station, a car, a taxi
h) fantastic, nice, awful

2 Check your answers with another student.

D Grammar quiz

Work in groups. Choose the correct answer; a, b or c. There's one point for each correct answer.

1 There are .... beautiful trees in this park.
   a) some   b) a   c) any

2 Janek's from Poland, and .... married.
   a) he's   b) his   c) he

3 "What are ...., Dad?"
   "They're vegetables."
   a) them   b) that   c) those

4 My friend Kemal is ....
   a) actor   b) a actor
   c) an actor

5 There are five .... in our family.
   a) childs   b) children
   c) childrens

6 The café is .... the post office.
   a) on the left   b) on left of
   c) on the left of

7 This is .... favourite café.
   a) he   b) her   c) him

8 Are there .... French students in your class?
   a) a   b) some   c) any

E Vocabulary

1 Write words in the space and find the question.

a) food from the sea
b) Tom Cruise is an ....
c) You .... with a pen.
d) What's your .... number?
e) not married
f) Sorry, I .... understand.
g) a very small child
h) a person from the USA is ....
i) plural of 'woman'
j) 50
k) .... at the picture on page 12.
l) "How .... is that?" "$25"

2 Write the answer to the question here ....

F Song – *Hello, Goodbye*

1 Match the words in the box with their opposites.

yes   stop   hello   high   low   no   go   goodbye

2 🔲 **[2] Listen and match the lines in the song.**

3 Listen again and check.

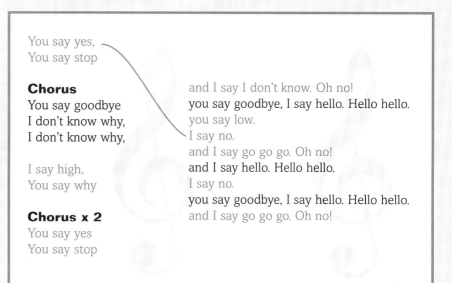

You say yes,
You say stop

Chorus
You say goodbye
I don't know why,
I don't know why,

I say high,
You say why

Chorus x 2
You say yes
You say stop

and I say I don't know. Oh no!
you say goodbye, I say hello. Hello hello.
you say low.
I say no.
and I say go go go. Oh no!
and I say hello. Hello hello.
I say no.
you say goodbye, I say hello. Hello hello.
and I say go go go. Oh no!

module 5
Home, work and family

▶ **Grammar:** Present Simple:
I and *you*; possessive *'s*
▶ **Vocabulary:** family members;
personal possessions
▶ **Real life:** in a shop

Focus 1

Vocabulary: family

1 Match the words with pictures 1–5.
▶ Vocabulary book page 22.

a) brother and sister – pictures 2 and 5
b) father and son
c) mother and daughter
d) parents and children
e) husband and wife
f) grandparents and grandchildren

2 [5.1] Listen and repeat.

3 Circle the odd one out.

a) son, parent, daughter
b) husband, wife, child
c) grandparent, brother, sister
d) brother, son, wife
e) wife, children, mother
f) sister, father, husband

Rosa

Tony

Possessive 's

4 a) Read the sentences and write the names on the picture.

- Carmen is Tony and Rosa's mother.
- Carlos is Carmen's husband and Rosa and Tony's father.
- Tony is Laura's husband.
- Luis and Marta are Tony and Laura's son and daughter.

b) Write the correct word.

a) Laura is Marta's ...mother............ .

b) Tony is Carmen's ....

c) Laura is Tony's ....

d) Carlos and Carmen are Rosa's ....

e) Luis is Marta's ....

f) Carlos and Carmen are Luis's ....

g) Marta and Luis are Tony and Laura's ....

5 🔲 [5.2] Listen and check.

Grammar

Possessive 's

Laura is Tony**'s** wife.

Not: ~~Laura is the wife of Tony.~~

Marta is Tony and Laura**'s** daughter.

▶ *Language summary 5A, page 115.*

Pronunciation

1 🔲 [5.3] Practise the sentences from Exercise 4b):

Marta's→Marta's mother→Laura is Marta's mother.

Carmen's→Carmen's son→Tony is Carmen's son.

6 Write more sentences about the family.

Tony is Marta's father.

a) Tony→Marta   e) Laura→Marta and Luis

b) Rosa→Carlos   f) Laura and Tony→Marta

c) Carlos→Carmen   g) Rosa→Tony

d) Tony→Carlos

Speaking task

1 Write the names of four people in your family.

2 Tell another student who they are.

> Marco's my brother. He's 26.

Don't forget!

"He's/She's from (*Rome*)."   "He's (*seventeen*)."

"She's (*an engineer*)."   "He's my (*father*)."

Carolina, 21, from Rosario in Argentina

Gabor, 25, from Budapest in Hungary

Focus 2

Vocabulary and reading

1 Match the verbs with the words in the box.

with computers   in a flat   a cat   a garden
languages   ~~with your parents~~

▶ Vocabulary book page 23.

live
- a) with your parents
- in the centre of the city
- in London
- b) ....
- alone

have
- two sisters
- three children
- c) ....
- d) ....

work
- for a big company
- e) ....
- in the centre of the city

study
- English
- a lot
- f) ....

2 🔊 [5.4] Listen and read. Match the pictures with the texts.

a " I live with my wife, Eva, and our baby daughter, near the centre of the city. I'm a medical student, and flats are very expensive in Budapest, so we live with my parents ... and my brother. The flat's quite small and there are a lot of people in it – sometimes it's very difficult. "

b " I live in a small flat in the centre of the city, and I work in the centre too, for a German bank. I don't live with my family – my parents live in Scotland. But I have a lot of friends here in Manchester, and I have six cats too, so I'm not really alone. "

c " I work with small children and I live very near the school, with my family. We're a big family – I have four brothers and a sister, but two of my brothers are married, so they don't live with my parents. We have a nice big house, with a beautiful garden. "

③

Louise, 33, from Manchester in England

Present Simple with *I*

3 Read the sentences. Who is speaking – Louise (L), Gabor (G) or Carolina (C)?

a) "I have a one-year-old daughter." ..G.......

b) "I don't have any brothers or sisters." ....

c) "I don't live in a flat."
....

d) "I work for a big company."
....

e) "I work in a school." ....

f) "I don't have a job." ....

g) "I study a lot." ....

h) "We have a big garden."
....

4 ▭ [5.5] Listen and check.

Grammar

Present Simple with *I:*

➕

I **work** in the centre of the city.   ➖   I **don't live** with my parents.
(= do not)

Present Simple with *you, we* and *they:*

They **live** in Scotland.   They **don't live** with my parents.
We **have a** big house.   You **don't have** a garden.

▶ *Language summary 5B, page 115.*

5 <u>Underline</u> the Present Simple verbs in the texts on page 42.

6 Rewrite the sentences in Exercise 3 to make them true for you. Compare your answers with a partner.

I don't have a one-year-old daughter!

Pronunciation

1 ▭ [5.6] Listen and repeat. Notice the stress:

live   I live with my parents.

work   I work with computers.

don't have   I don't have a garden.

don't live   I don't live alone.

don't study I don't study German.

Writing task

1 Write four of these sentences about yourself but do not write your name!

I live in …	I don't live in …
I have …	I don't have a/any …
I study …	I don't study …
I work in/with/for …	I don't work …

I live in Alexander Street. I have one brother, but I don't have any sisters. I study English and German. I don't work. WHO AM I?

2 Give your sentences to your teacher. Read your new sentences to the class. Who is it, do you think?

Focus 3

Present Simple questions

1 Read and answer the questionnaire.

2 Ask and answer questions 1–8 with a partner.

> ### Grammar
>
> Questions with *you*:
>
> Where **do** you **live**?
> **Do** you **live** in a flat?
>
> Short answers:
>
> Yes, I **do.**   No, I **don't.**
> ~~Yes, I live.~~   ~~No, I don't live.~~

3 Make more questions.

a Do you live in a big city?

a) live in a big city?
b) work with computers?
c) work in a big company?
d) study English in a school?
e) study any other languages?
f) have a car?
g) have a job?
h) have a dog?
i) work in the centre of town?
j) have any brothers or sisters?

> ### Pronunciation
>
> 1 [5.7] Listen and check. Notice that *do* is weak in the questions.
>   /dəjuː/
>   Do you live in a big city?
> 2 Practise the questions.

4 Talk to three students. Ask each student four questions from Exercise 3.

Do you work with computers?

No, I don't.

Home Life

1) **Do you live in the centre of town?** Yes, I do. ☐ No, I don't. ☐

2) **Do you live in a house or a flat?** a house ☐ a flat ☐

3) **Do you have a garden?** Yes, I do. ☐ No, I don't. ☐

4) **Who do you live with?** I live alone. ☐ friends ☐ my parents ☐ my husband/wife ☐

5) **How many people are there in your house?** 1–2 ☐ 3–4 ☐ 5–6 ☐ more ☐

6) **Do you have any children?** Yes, I do. ☐ No, I don't. ☐

7) **Do you have any pets?** Yes, I do. ☐ No I don't. ☐

8) **Do you work/study near your home?** Yes, I do. ☐ No, I don't. ☐ I work at home. ☐

Vocabulary: personal possessions

5 a) Match the words with the pictures.

a credit card   a passport   a radio   a watch
a magazine   glasses   a camera   a mobile phone
money   a purse   a wallet   a CD

▶ Vocabulary book page 24.

b) 🔊 [5.8] Listen and practise the words.

6 Which things does your partner have with him/her?

> Do you have a camera with you?

> No, I don't.

7 a) Whose are the things in the picture, do you think – Maggie's, Richard's or Ellen's?

mobile phone – Ellen's

b) Compare answers with a partner.

> I think the mobile phone is Ellen's.

> Yes, I think you're right.

c) 🔊 [5.9] Listen and check.

Maggie (age 75)

Richard, her son (age 47)

Ellen, Richard's daughter (age 15)

Listening

1   [5.10] Listen to an interview with Andy. Complete the form.

Phillips and Jones
Market Research

1 **Age:**

16–24	☐	25–34	☐
35–44	☐	45–55	☐
55 +	☐		

2 **Job:**

yes	☐	no	☐

3

male	☐	female	☐

4 **Possessions:**

computer	☐	PlayStation	☐
TV	☐	video	☐
DVD player	☐	CD player	☐
mobile phone	☐	camera	☐

5 **Credit cards:**

Mastercard	☐	Visa	☐
American Express	☐		

2 Work in pairs. Practise the interview.

Student A: You are Andy.

Student B: You are the interviewer.

Real life

In a shop

1 Look at the picture of a shop on page 47. Which things does the shop have?

postcards	stamps	newspapers
magazines	tissues	phone cards
cigarettes	lighters	

▶ Vocabulary book page 25.

2   [5.11] Silvia is in a shop. Listen and tick (✔) the things she buys.

3 **a)** Match the sentences in A and B. Silvia's sentences are in the **correct** order.

A Silvia

1 | d | Do you have any Italian newspapers?
2 | ☐ | Oh, OK. How much are the phone cards?
3 | ☐ | Can I have two? And these postcards, please.
4 | ☐ | Thanks. Do you have any stamps?
5 | ☐ | OK, thanks a lot. Bye.

B Shop assistant

a) Goodbye.

b) No, but there's a post office in the High Street.

c) Sure. That's £11.50, please.

d) No, sorry. We only have English newspapers.

e) They're five pounds.

b) Listen again and check. Practise Silvia's sentences.

4 Work with a partner. Have a conversation in a shop. Student A: Look at page 108. Student B: Look at page 110.

> Do you have any postcards?

> Yes, they're 30p.

Do you remember?

► Language summary, page 115
► Vocabulary book, pages 22–26

1 a) Circle the correct preposition.
a) I live *in/for* the centre of the city.
b) I don't live *in/with* a flat.
c) I don't live *in/with* my grandparents.
d) I work *in/with* a school.
e) I work *in/for* Microsoft.

b) Which sentences are true for you?

2 Write the words for personal possessions.
a) R A C A M E c.amera......
b) B O I L M E N E P H O m............ p.........
c) L A T E L W w.............
d) S L A G S S E g...............
e) D O I R A r..........
f) T E D C I R D A R C c.............. c.........

3 Put the words in the correct columns.

mother   grandchild   son   husband
child   father   grandparent   wife
sister   brother   parent   daughter

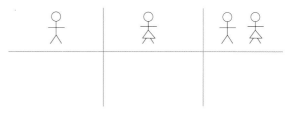

4 Match the sentences 1–6 with the answers a–f.
1) Do you have a cat?
2) What languages do you study?
3) Do you have any children?
4) Where do you live?
5) Who do you work for?
6) Do you live in a big house?

a) In San Salvador, a city in Brazil.
b) No, it's quite small.
c) English and Spanish.
d) No, but I have three dogs.
e) Yes, two boys and a girl.
f) ICI – it's a British company.

module 6

We both like ...

- ▶ **Grammar**: object pronouns; Present Simple: *he*, *she*, *it*
- ▶ **Vocabulary**: likes and dislikes; free time activities
- ▶ **Real life**: telling the time (1)

Focus 1

Vocabulary: likes and dislikes

1 **a)** Which things below are in the pictures?

rock music	classical music
Italian food	football
shopping	cooking
reading	dancing
a cartoon	

▶ Vocabulary book page 27.

b) 📼 [6.1] Listen and practise.

2 **a)** Put these phrases on the line.

> I hate ...   I don't like ...   I love ...   ...~~is/are okay~~   I like ...

☺☺   ☺   😐   ☹   ☹☹

is/are okay

b) Talk about the things in Exercise 1 in pairs.

I don't like shopping.

Classical music is okay.

Object pronouns: *him/her/it*

3 Find two answers to questions 1–4.

A	B
1 Do you like **Brad Pitt**?	a) **He**'s okay.
	b) Yes, **they**'re great!
2 Do you like **Madonna**?	c) No, I hate **it**.
	d) Yes, **she**'s great.
3 Do you like **cooking**?	e) No, I hate **them**!
	f) Yes, I really like **him**.
4 Do you like **cartoons**?	g) **It**'s okay.
	h) Yes, I love **her**.

Grammar

Subject pronouns	Object pronouns
~~Brad Pitt~~ He is okay.	I really like ~~Brad Pitt~~ him.
She is great.	I love **her**.
It is okay.	I like **it**.
They are great.	I hate **them**.

▶ *Language summary 6D, page 115.*

---

4 a) Circle the correct answer.

a) Do you like dancing? Yes, I love *it/him*.
b) Do you like cats? No, I hate *they/them*.
c) Do you like rock music? *It's/They're* okay.
d) Do you like Tom Cruise? Yes, I like *he/him* a lot.
e) Do you like Julia Roberts? No, I hate *she/her*!
f) Do you like reading in English? Yes, I love *it/them*!

b) 🔲 [6.2] Listen and check. Practise asking and answering the questions with a partner.

5 Ask your partner about these. Use a pronoun in your answer.

dogs	tea	babies	Jennifer Lopez	dance music	coffee
Chinese food		Elton John	supermarkets	vegetables	

> Do you like tea?

> Yes, it's okay.

Speaking task

1 Work with a new partner. Find six things you both like.

> Do you like football?

> Yes, I love it!

> Me, too. Do you like shopping?

2 Tell the class two things that you both like.

> We both like cartoons.

Don't forget!

Do you like	(*busy cities*)?
	(*tea with milk*)?
	(*dogs*)?

Me too.

We both like (*French food*).

49

Focus 2

Vocabulary and listening

1 Match the nouns with the correct verb.

> a computer game   a video
> a newspaper   the Internet
> ▶ Vocabulary book page 28.

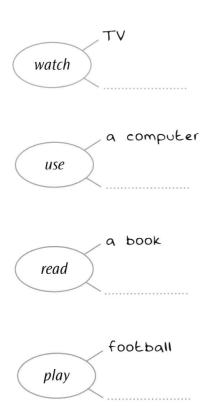

watch ─── TV
....

use ─── a computer
....

read ─── a book
....

play ─── football
....

2 **a)** Do you think sentences a–h in the table are true (T) or false (F)? If you don't know, write (?).

b) Compare answers with other students.

Emma   Simon

3 **a)** 🔲 [6.3] Listen to Emma and Simon. Which six things in the table do they talk about?

b) Listen again. Write true (T), false (F), or don't know (?) for Emma and Simon.

	you	Emma	Simon
a Most men don't like cooking.		T	?
b Most children don't like school.			
c Most children watch TV every day.			
d Most men don't like shopping.			
e Most women don't play computer games.			
f Most young people have a mobile phone.			
g Most old people don't use the Internet.			
h Most young people don't read newspapers.			

Present Simple: *he* and *she*

4  [6.4] What do Emma and Simon say?
Circle the correct words. Listen and check.

a) *My children/My friends* love school.

b) *My son/My daughter* watches a lot of TV.

c) *My brother/My husband* likes shopping too.

d) *My sister/My daughter* plays computer games a lot.

e) *My father/My mother* uses the Internet all the time.

> ### Grammar
>
> **Present Simple: *he* and *she***
>
> **He** like**s** shopping.
>
> **She** play**s** computer games a lot.
>
> **My son** watch**es** a lot of TV.
>
> Notice with *have:*
>
> My daughter **has** a mobile phone.
>
> ~~haves~~
>
> **Remember: They love** school.
>
> Not: ~~loves~~
>
> ▶ *Language summary 6, page 115.*

> ### Pronunciation
>
> 1  [6.5] Listen to the verbs. How many syllables, one or two? Listen again and repeat.
>
> reads   uses   likes   plays   looks   writes
>
> watches   lives   works   teaches

5 Write **ten** sentences about people you know. Use the ideas in the diagram.

My brother watches TV every day.
My parents like classical music.

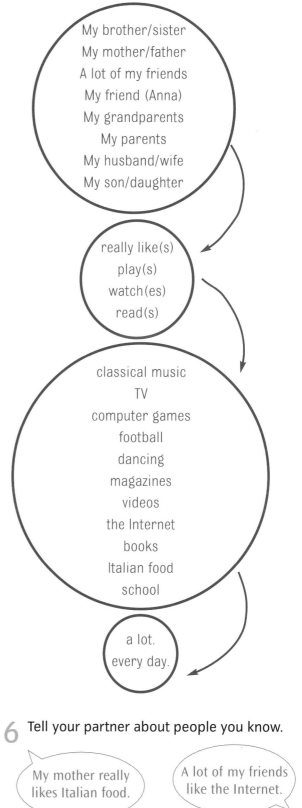

> My brother/sister
> My mother/father
> A lot of my friends
> My friend (Anna)
> My grandparents
> My parents
> My husband/wife
> My son/daughter

> really like(s)
> play(s)
> watch(es)
> read(s)

> classical music
> TV
> computer games
> football
> dancing
> magazines
> videos
> the Internet
> books
> Italian food
> school

> a lot.
> every day.

6 Tell your partner about people you know.

> My mother really likes Italian food.

> A lot of my friends like the Internet.

Focus 3

Reading and vocabulary

1 Look at the photos but don't read. There are three couples. Who do you think is with who?

2 Check the words in **bold**. Read about the three women and complete the sentences.

▶ Vocabulary book page 29.

a) ..Melanie... loves **animals**.
b) .... doesn't **eat** meat.
c) .... works in the **theatre**.
d) .... **speaks** five languages.
e) .... loves **travelling**.
f) .... works in a **hospital**.
g) .... loves **sport**.

Questions: *he* and *she*

3 **a)** Match the questions with the answers in the box.

1 Does Melanie like dancing?
2 Does Isabel eat meat?
3 Does Nicole like music?

We don't know.	No, she doesn't.
Yes, she does.	

b) 🔊 [6.6] Listen and check. Practise the questions and answers.

> ### Grammar
>
> Questions: *he* and *she*
> ❓ **Does** Melanie **like** dancing?
>   like~~s~~
> Yes, she **does**.
> No, she **doesn't**.
>
> ▶ *Language summary 6C, page 115.*

Isabel

Age: 29

Job: teaches languages at London University

Loves: languages (she speaks five), reading, travelling, jazz, shopping, the cinema

Hates: meat, football

Nicole

Age: 22

Job: nurse in children's hospital

Loves: children, the Internet, all sport, especially playing tennis

Hates: dogs, cooking

Melanie

Age: 27

Job: theatre manager

Loves: rock music, eating, dancing, children, all animals

Hates: all sport, computer games

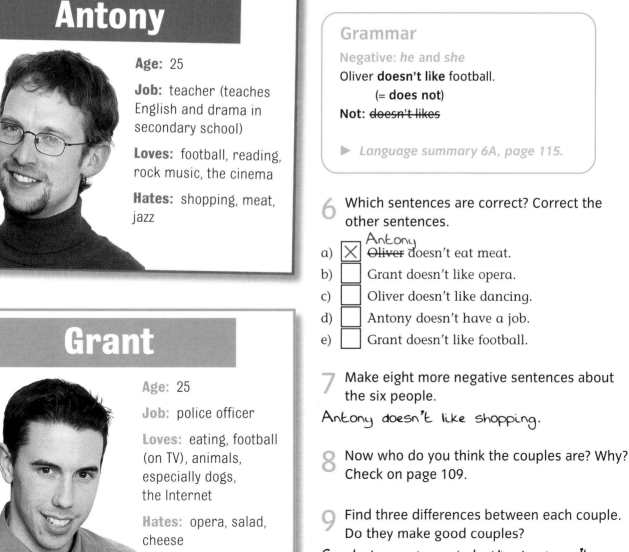

Oliver

Age: 28

Job: student

Loves: the theatre, all music (rock, jazz, classical), playing computer games

Hates: dancing, football, babies

Antony

Age: 25

Job: teacher (teaches English and drama in secondary school)

Loves: football, reading, rock music, the cinema

Hates: shopping, meat, jazz

Grant

Age: 25

Job: police officer

Loves: eating, football (on TV), animals, especially dogs, the Internet

Hates: opera, salad, cheese

---

4 Put the questions in order. Ask and answer with a partner.

Does Melanie like computer games?

a) Does/like/computer games/Melanie ?

b) Isabel/read/Does/a lot ?

c) cooking/Does/like/Nicole ?

d) Isabel/Does/work/with children ?

e) Nicole/computer games/play/Does ?

5 Read about the three men. Ask and answer questions with a partner. Use these phrases:

a) like football   c) eat meat

b) have a job   d) read a lot

Does Oliver like football?

Negative: *he* and *she*

> ### Grammar
> Negative: *he* and *she*
>
> Oliver **doesn't like** football.
>   (= **does not**)
> **Not:** ~~doesn't likes~~
>
> ▶ *Language summary 6A, page 115.*

6 Which sentences are correct? Correct the other sentences.

a) ☒ ~~Oliver~~ *Antony* doesn't eat meat.

b) ☐ Grant doesn't like opera.

c) ☐ Oliver doesn't like dancing.

d) ☐ Antony doesn't have a job.

e) ☐ Grant doesn't like football.

7 Make eight more negative sentences about the six people.

Antony doesn't like shopping.

8 Now who do you think the couples are? Why? Check on page 109.

9 Find three differences between each couple. Do they make good couples?

Grant loves dogs, but Nicole doesn't like them.

Speaking task

1 Walk around the class. Find one person in the class who:

- doesn't like cats. ....
- speaks two (or more) foreign languages. ....
- reads a lot. ....
- lives near your school. ....
- doesn't like rock music. ....
- doesn't play computer games. ....
- plays football a lot. ....
- doesn't watch TV. ....
- likes opera. ....
- doesn't like babies. ....

2 Tell the class your answers.

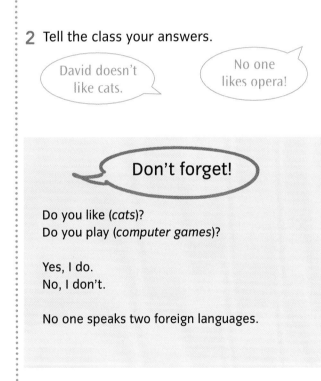

> David doesn't like cats.

> No one likes opera!

Don't forget!

Do you like (*cats*)?
Do you play (*computer games*)?

Yes, I do.
No, I don't.

No one speaks two foreign languages.

Real life

Telling the time (1)

1 [6.7] Listen and practise the times.

2 a) [6.8] Listen and draw the times, like this.

b) Ask and answer about the times in 2a).

> What time is it?

> It's seven o'clock.

3 Write the answers.

a) What time does your English lesson start?
   At half past ten.

b) What time does it finish?

c) What time does your school open every day?

d) What time do shops open in your country? What time do they close?

e) What time do banks open? What time do they close?

Do you remember?

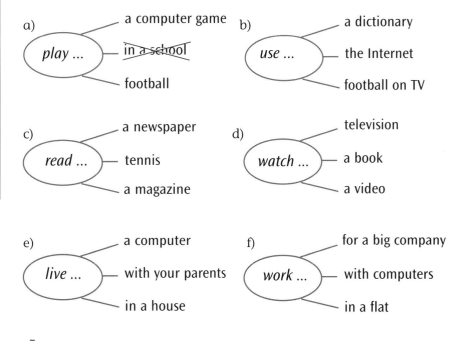

4 🔲 [6.9] Listen and (circle) the time you hear.

(a)

seven o'clock   eight o'clock
eleven o'clock

(b)

quarter to eight
quarter past eight
half past eight

(c)

quarter to six   quarter past six
half past six

(d)

quarter to three
quarter past three
half past three

▶ Language summary, page 115
▶ Vocabulary book, pages 27–31

1 Add **-s** or **-es** or nothing (Ø)
a) Tim really like classical music.
b) My sisters love shopping.
c) His brother watch videos a lot.
d) I use a computer when I'm at work.
e) She read the newspaper every day.
f) Frank teach English at university.

2 a) (Circle) the correct word.
a) (Do)/Does you like cats or dogs?
b) Do/Does you eat meat?
c) Do/Does your best friend have a computer?
d) Do/Does you play tennis or football?
e) Do/Does your brothers and sisters live near you?
f) Do/Does your English teacher speak your language?

b) Ask and answer the questions with a partner.

3 Cross out the phrase in the wrong place in a–f.

a) play ...
— a computer game
— ~~in a school~~
— football

b) use ...
— a dictionary
— the Internet
— football on TV

c) read ...
— a newspaper
— tennis
— a magazine

d) watch ...
— television
— a book
— a video

e) live ...
— a computer
— with your parents
— in a house

f) work ...
— for a big company
— with computers
— in a flat

4 Find the seven pairs of opposites.

| (open) | hate | expensive | small | hot | start | left |
| cheap | love | cold | finish | (close) | big | right |

55

Your time

▶ **Grammar:** adverbs of frequency
▶ **Vocabulary:** daily routines; time expressions; days of the week
▶ **Real life:** telling the time (2)

Focus 1

Vocabulary: daily routines

1 **a)** Match these phrases with pictures 1–10.

▶ Vocabulary book page 32.

go to bed **9**	have dinner
finish work	get home
start work	have lunch
go to work	get up **1**
have breakfast	sleep

b) 🔊 [7.1] Listen and check.

2 What do people usually do:

a) in the morning?   *get up*

b) in the afternoon?

c) in the evening?

d) at night?

56

Reading

3 Look at the photos on the right. What are Susannah and Marcus's jobs?

4 Read the text. Who is talking – Susannah or Marcus?

" My daily routine? Well, … I sleep all morning, and I get up at about one in the afternoon. I love getting up late, when all my friends are at work! Then at about one thirty I go to a café for breakfast. After that … well, I go shopping to buy some new records. And in the evening … I usually go to work at about half past nine and start work at ten thirty. I enjoy my job so it isn't really work. I love watching people dance to the music. The club closes at three, and I get home at about quarter past four. I go to bed at about five in the morning – I'm usually really tired by then, but I know that I have the best job in the world! "

Marcus is a DJ in a London club.

Susannah is a violinist in an orchestra.

5 ⬜ [7.2] Read the text again and listen. Write sentences for these times.

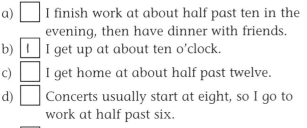

He sleeps in the morning.

a) in the morning
b) 1.00 p.m.
c) 1.30 p.m.
d) in the afternoon
e) 9.30 p.m.
f) 10.30 p.m.
g) 4.15 a.m.
h) 5.00 a.m.

6 ⬜ [7.3] Read about Susannah. Put the sentences in order. Listen and check.

a) ☐ I finish work at about half past ten in the evening, then have dinner with friends.
b) ☐ 1 I get up at about ten o'clock.
c) ☐ I get home at about half past twelve.
d) ☐ Concerts usually start at eight, so I go to work at half past six.
e) ☐ I usually have breakfast in the garden.
f) ☐ Then I watch TV or read a book, and go to bed at about two o'clock in the morning.
g) ☐ I have lunch at about two, and then practise in the afternoon.

Speaking task

1 Look at the pictures on page 56. What time do **you** do these things?

get up – eight o'clock

2 Work with a partner. Ask questions about the things in Exercise 1.

What time do you get up?

At half past seven. And you?

Don't forget!

What time do you (*have lunch*)?

At (about) one o'clock.

I don't (*have dinner*).

Focus 2

Vocabulary: days of the week

1 a) 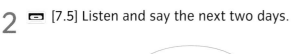 [7.4] Put the days of the week in order. Listen and check.

	Tuesday		Wednesday
	Friday		Thursday
	Sunday	1	Monday
	Saturday		

b) Listen again and mark the stress. Practise saying the words.

Mónday

▶ Vocabulary book page 33.

2 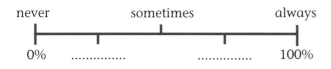 [7.5] Listen and say the next two days.

Monday, Tuesday ...
(Wednesday, Thursday)

Adverbs of frequency

3 a) Look at the adverbs of frequency. Put *usually* and *not usually* in the correct place.

never   sometimes   always

├──────┼──────────┼──────────┼──────┤

0% 100%

b) Are these sentences true or false for **your** country?

a) Children **always** start school before 9 o'clock.

b) Cinemas **usually** open in the morning.

c) Shops **sometimes** close for lunch.

d) Children **don't usually** go to school on Saturdays.

e) Banks **never** open on Sundays.

4 Change the adverbs in sentences a–e in Exercise 3b) to make them true for **your** country. Compare your sentences with a partner.

(In France, shops usually close for lunch.)

Grammar

Adverbs of frequency

Notice the word order:

    1   2   3
Shops **sometimes** close in the afternoon.

    1   2   3   4
Children **don't usually** go to school on Saturdays.

▶ *Language summary 7, page 116.*

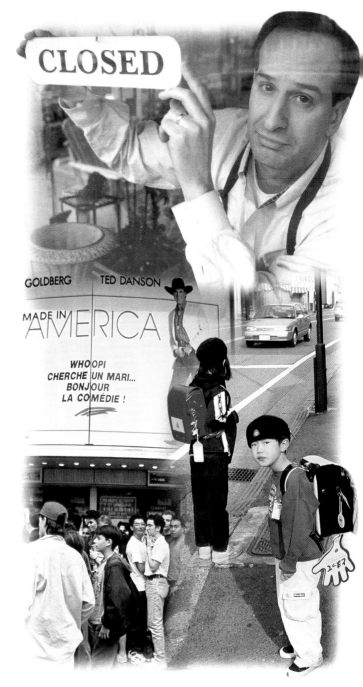

Mansoor is from Dubai.

Justine is from France.

Listening

5 **a)** Write the correct adverb for your country in sentences a–f below.

Example: a – sometimes

b) Compare your answers with other students.

6 **a)** ▭ [7.6] Listen to Mansoor and Justine. Which things below do they talk about?

Example: Mansoor – a

b) Listen again. Write the adverbs they use for each sentence.

7 Write three **true** sentences and one **false** sentence about life in Dubai or France. Tell your partner.

> In Dubai, people always wear shoes in the house.

> False!

8 Make true sentences about **you**. Compare with a partner.

I never sleep in the afternoon.

a) sleep in the afternoon
b) eat meat for breakfast
c) drink coffee in the evening
d) go to bed after 1 a.m.
e) get up early on Sundays
f) watch TV in the morning
g) walk to work/school
h) watch sport on TV

In my country ...

a people .... have tea with breakfast.

b people .... wear shoes in the house.

c people .... have a big lunch.

d people .... sleep in the afternoon.

e people .... kiss their friends when they meet.

f people .... have dinner at 10 p.m.

Focus 3
Reading and speaking

1 🔊 [7.7] Match words and phrases in a and b. Listen and check.

(a) meet   go to   read   do   stay   watch
listen to   clean

(b) in   a book   friends   TV   the cinema
music   your homework   the house

▶ Vocabulary book page 34.

2 Do the magazine quiz. Choose the **best** answer for you.

3 **a)** Ask and answer questions 1–6 with a partner.

b) Count how many a's, b's and c's your partner has. Now look at page 112.

How **free** is your free time?

1 What do you usually do in the evening?
a   I have dinner, watch TV and go to bed early!
b   Sometimes I go to a restaurant or to the cinema, sometimes I stay in.
c   I usually go to a club or meet friends in town.

2 What time do you go to bed on Friday night?
a   At about eleven o'clock – I'm always tired on Friday night.
b   At about one or two o'clock in the morning.
c   I don't usually go to bed on Friday night!

3 What do you usually do on Saturday?
a   I clean the house and go to the supermarket.
b   I go shopping, listen to music or watch sport on TV.
c   I sleep all day, after Friday night!

4 When do you cook?
a   Every evening for my family.
b   I cook for friends at the weekend.
c   I never cook – I buy a burger if I'm hungry.

5 When and what do you read?
a   I sometimes read the newspaper in the evening ... if I have time.
b   I read a book in bed at night.
c   I don't read a lot – I'm usually out with my friends.

6 When do you do your English homework?
a   Half an hour before the lesson.
b   At the weekend, when I have lots of time.
c   I don't usually do my English homework!

Time expressions

4 Look at these examples then put the words and phrases in the correct spaces.

> the afternoon   Wednesday   half past ten
> the evening   day   quarter past four
> Sunday   week
>
> ▶ Vocabulary book page 34.

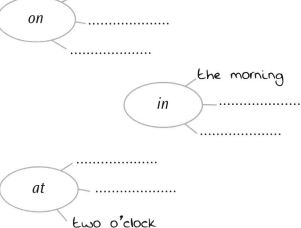

Saturday
on ....
....

in the morning ....
....

at ....
....
two o'clock

every weekend ....
....

5 Test your partner.

the morning   in the morning

6 a) Circle the correct preposition.

a) Do you study English *in/at/every* day?

b) Are you usually at home *at/in/on* nine o'clock *in/on/at* the morning?

c) Do you go to the cinema *in/on/every* week?

d) What do you do *in/on/at* the weekend?

e) Do you read the newspaper *in/every/on* day?

f) What do you usually do *in/on/at* Friday?

g) Are you usually at home *on/at/every* five o'clock *in/on/at* the afternoon?

b) Ask and answer questions a–g with a partner.

Speaking task

1 Write **six** questions to interview your teacher about his/her daily routine and free time.

2 With other students, ask your teacher the questions.

Don't forget!

Do you (usually) (*visit friends at the weekend*)?

When do you (*clean the house*)?

Do you like (*dancing*)?

What time do you (*get up*)?

What do you usually do on (*Saturday*)?

Writing

7 a) Write a paragraph about your daily routine and free time. Don't write your name!

> I usually get up at about eight o'clock, and start work at nine. At the weekend I sometimes go to the cinema, and I sometimes go to my friend's house. On Sunday, I usually ...

b) Read about other students' daily routines. Guess the names of the students.

Real life

Telling the time (2)

1 **a)** Write the times.

(a)

(b)

five past eight ....

.... past two

(c)

(d)

.... six

....

(e)

(f)

twenty-five to one ....

twenty .... four

(g)

(h)

.... nine

....

b) 🖭 [7.8] Listen and check. Practise saying the times.

2 **a)** 🖭 [7.9] Circle the time you hear.

a) 3.40   (4.20)   e) 6.40   6.20

b) 2.10   1.50   f) 8.35   9.25

c) 9.55   10.05   g) 2.50   3.10

d) 7.35   8.25

b) Say a time from Exercise 2a). Your partner points to the number.

3 🖭 [7.10] Louise and Greg want to watch TV. Listen and write the time these programmes are on.

Programme	Time
The News	
George Michael in Concert	
Titanic	
Casablanca	
Football Night	

4 Ask and answer questions about television times.

Student B: Turn to page 111.

Student A: Ask your partner what time the programmes start, and write the times.

What time does *House and Garden* start?

Ten to eight.

BBC 1

.... **House and Garden**
 8.25 **Holiday!**
.... **The BBC News**
10.35 **Dracula**

BBC 2

 7.35 **The Simpsons**
.... **Sports World**
 9.40 **The X Files**
.... **Newsnight**

ITV

.... **Star Wars**
 9.30 **The Doctors**
.... **ITV Evening News**
10.35 **Elton John in concert**

CHANNEL 4

 7.00 **Channel Four News**
.... **Go Shopping!**
 8.40 **Friends**
.... **The Day Today**

Do you remember?

► Language summary, page 116
► Vocabulary book, pages 32–36

1 Circle the correct answer.
a) When do you *have/go* lunch?
b) I usually *go to/go* the cinema on Saturday evening.
c) My husband *goes to/gets* home at about six.
d) What time do you *go/get up* in the morning?
e) I *have/start* work at half past nine every day.
f) What time does your sister *get/leave* work?

2 a) Put the words in the correct order.
a) get up/usually/I/eight o'clock/before
   I usually get up before eight o'clock.
b) I/breakfast/have/usually/don't
c) shopping/sometimes/I/on Sunday/go
d) watch/at the weekend/I/sport/always/on TV
e) before/I/nine o'clock/home/leave/never

b) Tick the sentences that are true for you. Compare answers with a partner.

3 Write a day in the gaps. Compare answers with a partner.
a) Today is ....
b) Tomorrow is ....
c) My favourite day is ....
d) A day I don't like is ....
e) I study English on .... and ....
f) I get up late on ....

4 Draw the times on the clocks.

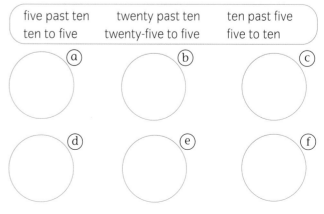

| five past ten | twenty past ten | ten past five |
| ten to five | twenty-five to five | five to ten |

ⓐ   ⓑ   ⓒ

ⓓ   ⓔ   ⓕ

module 8
People are amazing

- ▶ **Grammar:** *can/can't;*
  wh- questions
- ▶ **Vocabulary:** parts of the body;
  quantities
- ▶ **Real life:** big numbers

Focus 1

can and *can't*

1 Check the words in **bold**.
  ▶ Vocabulary book page 37.

a) He can **run** 100 metres in ten seconds.

b) She can't **walk**, but she can **play basketball** very well.

c) She's only ten but she can **play chess** really well.

d) He can **play the guitar** brilliantly, but he can't read music.

2 Match sentences a–d with the pictures.

Grammar

can and *can't*

I/you	**can** play chess. ⊕
He/She	**can't** read music. ⊖
We/They	(= **cannot**)

▶ *Language summary 8A, page 116.*

Pronunciation

1 ▭ [8.1] Listen to the pronunciation of *can* and *can't.*

/kən/ /kɑːnt/
He can run. He can't run.

2 ▭ [8.2] Listen and write the sentences you hear. Practise saying them.

3 a) Check the new verbs below.

▶ Vocabulary book page 37.

b) Use the verbs to make sentences about the children in the pictures.

A new baby can't stand.
A seven-year-old child can usually read and write.

A new baby

see   hear   sit   stand   eat food

A three-year-old child

walk   talk   run   read   write

A seven-year-old child

swim   ride a bicycle
use a computer   play chess

Questions with *can*

4 Tick (✓) the things you **can** do, and cross (✗) the things you **can't** do.

a) drive

b) run fast

c) swim 100 metres

d) play chess

e) cook well

f) read music

g) ride a bicycle

h) speak a foreign language

i) play the violin

j) write with your left hand

Grammar

Questions with *can*

Question:	**Can** you **drive**?
Short answers:	Yes, I **can**. 
	No, I **can't**.

▶ *Language summary 8A, page 116.*

---

5 Ask your partner about the things in Exercise 4.

Can you drive?   Can you run fast?

6 ▭ [8.3] Listen to Ben and Karis. What can Ben do? What can Karis do?

Speaking task

1 Work with a partner. Find three things that you can do but your partner can't do.

2 Tell the class.

Don't forget!

use the Internet   cook

speak (*French*)   dance

I can read music, but Carmen can't.

Focus 2

Vocabulary: the body

1 Point to these things on the picture of the human body.

> head   eye   hand   ear   foot (plural: feet)
> bone   arm   leg   blood
>
> ▶ Vocabulary book page 38.

2 ▭ [8.4] Listen and practise the words.

You're amazing!

1▶ You are one centimetre taller in the morning than in the evening.

10▶ An adult can see 10,000 different colours.

9▶ A new baby can't see colours.

8▶ Every litre of our blood travels 90,000 kilometres in our body.

7▶ We can live without water for about twelve days.

6▶ 50% of the bones in your body are in your hands and feet.

5▶ A new baby has 306 bones in its body. An adult has 206 bones.

Reading and listening

3 a) Read the facts (1–10) about the body. Which two are **not** true?

b) Compare your answers with other students.

Number 2 isn't true.

Are you sure?

4 a) 🎧 [8.5] Listen to Professor Klein and check the answers to Exercise 3.

b) Which facts do you think are amazing?

Professor Susan Klein

2 ▶ **We can live without food for about two months.**

3 ▶ **An adult eats about 200 kilos of food every year.**

4 ▶ **Our bodies are about 70% water.**

Vocabulary: *metres, minutes, kilos*

5 a) Put these words on the correct line, from small to big.

> a kilo   25%   a minute   a metre
> a kilometre   an hour   80%
>
> ▶ Vocabulary book page 39.

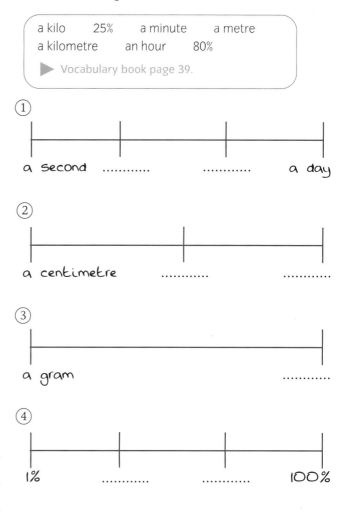

① a second .... a day

② a centimetre ....

③ a gram ....

④ 1% 100%

b) 🎧 [8.6] Listen and check.

> **Pronunciation**
>
> 1 🎧 [8.6] Listen again and mark the stress. Practise saying the words.
> second   centimetre   one per cent

Focus 3

Reading and listening

1 Read the caption about Jack Warren. What is his job?

2 Match questions 1–6 below with the answers a–f.

3 📼 [8.7] Listen and check your answers.

Jack Warren is an astronaut on the American Space Shuttle. He sometimes lives in space for several months.

I	c	How many astronauts are there on the Space Shuttle?
2		Where do you sleep?
3		When do you sleep?
4		What can you do in your free time?
5		Who do you talk to on Earth?
6		Why do you like working in space?

a) We talk to the people at **NASA** every day, and sometimes we can talk to our families.

b) Because it's a very interesting job, and it's very beautiful up there.

c) Sometimes there are four, sometimes seven.

d) We play cards, read books – or we can go for a spacewalk!

e) There aren't any beds, so we sleep in special sleeping bags.

f) There is no night or day in space, so we sleep when it is nighttime in America.

Wh- questions

1 Match question words 1–6 with a–f.

1	**What**?	a)	a person
2	**Who**?	b)	a place
3	**Where**?	c)	a time
4	**When**?	d)	a thing
5	**Why**?	e)	a number
6	**How many**?	f)	a reason

2 Notice the word order:

Where	**do**	**you**	sleep?
What	**can**	**you**	do in your free time?
How many	**are**	**there?**	

▶ *Language summary 8B, page 116.*

4 Read about Jack's normal life. Circle the correct question word.

Q1: Where/Why do you work when you're not on the Space Shuttle?

JACK: At NASA, in Florida.

Q2: *When/Where* do you live?

JACK: In Orlando, Florida.

Q3: *Who/What* do you live with?

JACK: My wife and children.

Q4: *What/Who* 's your wife's name?

JACK: Beth.

Q5: *What/When* 's her job?

JACK: She works at NASA too.

Q6: *What/How* many children do you have?

JACK: Two.

Q7: *How many/How old* are your children?

JACK: They're seven and five.

Q8: *Why/When* do you like working at NASA?

JACK: Because every day we learn something new.

5 Make questions.

a) do/you/What/do/at the weekend ?

   What do you do at the weekend?

b) your/'s/What/book or film/favourite ?

c) Who/favourite/singer/your/'s ?

d) go to bed/When/you/do ?

e) Where/go/do/for your holidays/you ?

f) people/How many/there/are/in your family ?

g) 's/favourite TV programme/your/What ?

Pronunciation

1 ▭ [8.8] Listen. We stress the important words.

a) What ... do ... weekend?
   What do you do at the weekend?

b) What ... favourite book?
   What's your favourite book?

c) Who ... favourite singer?
   Who's your favourite singer?

d) When ... go ... bed?
   When do you go to bed?

e) Where ... go ... holidays?
   Where do you go for your holidays?

2 Listen again and practise.

6 Ask a partner five questions from Exercise 5.

Who's your favourite singer?

Ricky Martin.

What's your favourite film?

Casablanca!

Real life

Big numbers

1 Write the numbers in the gaps.

> ~~a thousand~~   a million   ten thousand
> a hundred   a hundred thousand
> ▶ Vocabulary book page 40.

100 ....   1,000 _a thousand_
10,000 ....   100,000 ....
1,000,000 ....

2 ▭ [8.9] How do you say these numbers? Listen and (circle) the correct answer.

a) 100   (a hundred)/hundred
b) 300   three hundreds/three hundred
c) 150   a hundred and fifty/hundred fifty
d) 275   two hundreds and seventy-five/
              two hundred and seventy-five
e) 1,000   thousand/a thousand
f) 20,000   twenty thousand/twenty thousands

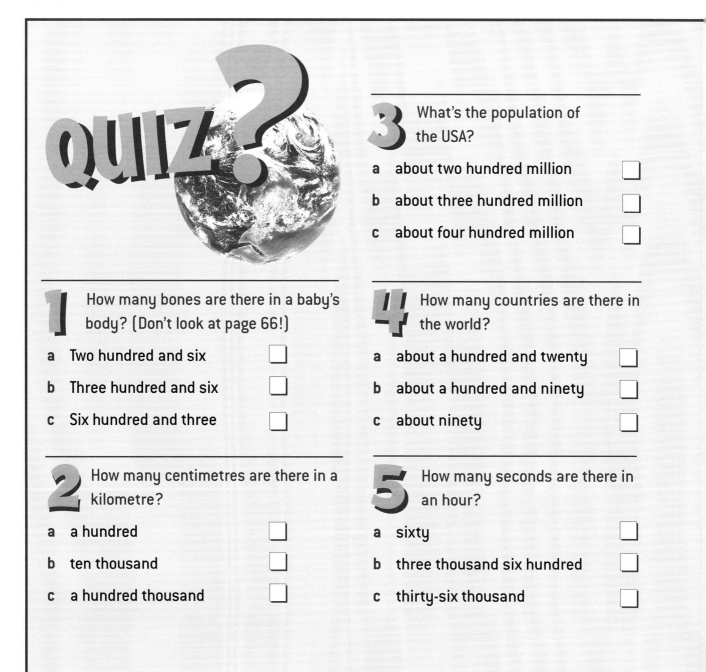

QUIZ?

3 What's the population of the USA?

a about two hundred million ☐

b about three hundred million ☐

c about four hundred million ☐

1 How many bones are there in a baby's body? (Don't look at page 66!)

a Two hundred and six ☐

b Three hundred and six ☐

c Six hundred and three ☐

4 How many countries are there in the world?

a about a hundred and twenty ☐

b about a hundred and ninety ☐

c about ninety ☐

2 How many centimetres are there in a kilometre?

a a hundred ☐

b ten thousand ☐

c a hundred thousand ☐

5 How many seconds are there in an hour?

a sixty ☐

b three thousand six hundred ☐

c thirty-six thousand ☐

Do you remember?

▶ Language summary, page 116
▶ Vocabulary book, pages 37– 41

3 🔊 [8.10] Listen and write the numbers.

1 7,000,000

4 a) Do the quiz in teams. Which team is the first to finish?

b) Check your answers on page 109.

---

6 How many kilometres is the Moon from the Earth?

a about forty thousand ☐

b about four hundred thousand ☐

c about four million ☐

---

7 How many pages are there in this book? (Don't look!)

a about a hundred and thirty ☐

b about two hundred ☐

c about two hundred and fifty ☐

---

1 There are 13 verbs in this box. Can you find them?

R	O	P	S	E	E	W
E	S	L	S	G	S	A
W	W	A	L	K	T	H
R	I	Y	R	E	A	D
I	M	S	I	T	N	U
T	A	L	K	E	D	S
E	M	H	E	A	R	E
R	U	N	L	T	A	G

2 a) Write four **true** sentences and two **false** sentences about you. Use *can* and *can't*.

I can't swim. I can play the guitar.

b) Say the sentences to another student. Can he/she guess which two are false?

3 a) Choose the correct question word.

(What   When   Where   Why   Who   How many)

a) .... brothers and sisters do you have?
b) .... 's your birthday?
c) .... do you usually do in the evening?
d) .... 's your favourite actor?
e) .... do your parents live?
f) .... do you want to learn English?

b) Work with a partner. Ask and answer the questions.

4 What are these parts of the body?

a) **R A E** = e.ar........   f) **T O F O** = f............
b) **D E H A** = h............   g) **E N O B** = b............
c) **E E Y** = e............   h) **D O L O B** = b............
d) **R A M** = a............   i) **D H A N** = h............
e) **G L E** = l............

Consolidation
modules 5–8

A Grammar: Present Simple

1 Read about Carol and her brother Eddie. Circle the correct answers.

"My brother Eddie and I are very different. He
a) *love/ loves* dance music, but I like classical music.
I b) *don't/ doesn't* like sport, but he loves it – he
c) *play/ plays* football every week. I never
d) *eat/ eats* meat, but he eats burgers every day. He usually gets up late, and I
e) *get up/ gets up* at six o'clock. But we both
f) *like/ likes* using the Internet, and he
g) *send/ sends* me emails every week."

"My sister Carol and I are very different. I really
h) *like/ likes* sport, especially football, but she
i) *don't/ doesn't* like it at all. Carol never
j) *eat/ eats* meat, but I eat it all the time. She
k) *get up/ gets up* really early, and I usually get up
at about eleven. She loves classical music, and I
l) *hate/ hates* it! But we both use the Internet a lot –
I send her emails every day – and we both
m) *love/ loves* dance music."

2 There are three differences in the texts. Can you find them? Compare your answers with a partner.

B Listening and speaking

1 🎧 [1] Listen to Tony talking about his friend Max. Circle the correct information about Max in the box below.

Name: (Max) /Mark
Nationality: English/American
Lives: in Turkey/in England
Job: doctor/teacher
Age: 29/39
Married: yes/no

2 Listen again and decide if these sentences about Max are true (T) or false (F).
a) Max hates computers. T
b) He works in a university.
c) He likes living in Izmir.
d) He lives in a big house.
e) He goes to concerts a lot.
f) He can play the guitar well.
g) He hates cooking.

C Grammar quiz

1 Work in teams. Choose the correct answer: a, b or c. There's one point for each correct answer.

1 Where .... he live?
   a) is   b) does   c) do
2 .... people are there in his family?
   a) What   b) Who   c) How many
3 Does he .... or study?
   a) work   b) job   c) works
4 What .... in his free time?
   a) he does   b) does he do   c) he does do
5 Does he .... sport?
   a) plays   b) like   c) watches
6 What .... at the weekend?
   a) does he usually do   b) usually does he do
   c) he usually does
7 What time does he get up .... the morning?
   a) in   b) on   c) at
8 .... any foreign languages?
   a) He can speak b) Can he speaks
   c) Can he speak

2 Work in pairs. Ask your partner the questions in the quiz about his/her friend.

D Vocabulary

Work in pairs. Complete the sentences with words from Modules 5–8.

1 The human body is **a** mazing.
2 I'm his sister, and he's my **b** _ _ _ _ _ _.
3 Do you use a **c** _ _ _ _ _ card when you go shopping?
4 We always have **d** _ _ _ _ _ at 8 p.m.
5 Sue often works in the **e** _ _ _ _ _ _.
6 Do you live in a house or a **f** _ _ _?
7 I can't read this. Where are my **g** _ _ _ _ _ _?
8 I'm his wife, and he's my **h** _ _ _ _ _ _.
9 Kingston is a very **i** _ _ _ _ _ _ _ _ _ _ city.
10 I like classical music, opera and **j** _ _ _.
11 I walk about five **k** _ _ _ _ _ _ _ _ _ every day.
12 I usually have **l** _ _ _ _ at one o'clock.
13 About 58 **m** _ _ _ _ _ _ people live in the UK.
14 I **n** _ _ _ _ watch cartoons. I hate them!
15 What time does the school **o** _ _ _?
16 My son **p** _ _ _ _ computer games every day.
17 It's **q** _ _ _ _ _ _ past ten.
18 I usually listen to the **r** _ _ _ _ when I get up.
19 My father **s** _ _ _ _ _ ten hours every night!
20 Tim's an actor, and he works in the **t** _ _ _ _ _ _.
21 What time do you **u** _ _ _ _ _ _ get up?

22 We sometimes watch a **v** _ _ _ _ on Friday evening.
23 Most men put their money in a **w** _ _ _ _ _.
24 _ **x** _ _ _ _ me, where's the station?
25 I play tennis _ _ _ _ **y** weekend.
26 I don't read books, I read _ _ _ _ **z** _ _ _ _.

E Song – *Eight days a week*

1 Write the days of the week and put them in order.

a) D M Y N O A ...Monday... 1
b) A S E E D D Y N W ....
c) A R A D U S Y T ....
d) D A N Y U S ....
e) T A D U S E Y ....
f) Y D T A R U S H ....
g) D R A I Y F ....

2 🔊 [2] Listen to the song and choose the correct words.

Ooh, I need your **love/kisses** babe.
Guess/Think you know it's true.
Hope you **need/want** my love babe,
Just like I need **you/it**.

Chorus
Hold me, love me, hold me, love me.
Ain't got nothin' but love babe,
Eight days a week.

Love you ev'ry **day/week** girl,
Usually/Always on my mind.
One thing I can **say/know** girl,
Love you **all the time/every day**.

Repeat Chorus

Eight days a week,
I **love/want** you.
Eight days a week,
Is not enough to **tell you/show** I care.

Ooh, I **need/have** your love babe,
Guess/Think you know it's true...

module 9

Now and then

▶ **Grammar:** Past Simple of *be*
▶ **Vocabulary:** common adjectives
▶ **Real life:** years; *When were you born?*

Focus 1

Common adjectives

1 Look at the photos. Which show the world:
– a hundred years ago?
– now?

2 Find these things in the pictures.

> **young** people   **poor** people
> **new** buildings   a **busy** road
> **happy** children   a **slow** car
> a **beautiful** place
> a **dangerous** road
>
> ▶ Vocabulary book page 42.

3 a) In the box find opposites for the adjectives in **bold** above.

> quiet   rich   old
> fast   safe   ugly
> unhappy   old
>
> ▶ Vocabulary book page 42.

young – old

b) 🔊 [9.1] Listen and check. Practise saying the adjectives.

4 Work with a partner.
Use the adjectives to
describe the pictures.

This road is
very quiet.

These people
are very poor.

5 **a)** Answer the questions.

1) Think of:
a) a cold country. Canada
b) a rich country.
c) a hot country.

2) In your country, think of:
a) a beautiful town.
b) a busy town.
c) a very old town.

3) In your town, think of:
a) a dangerous road.
b) a quiet road.
c) a cheap shop.

4) Think of:
a) a fast car.
b) a safe car.
c) an expensive car.

5) Think of a famous person
who is:
a) very old.
b) very young.
c) very ugly.

6) Think of a person in a
book (or on TV) who is:
a) very poor.
b) usually happy.
c) always unhappy.

b) Compare answers with a
partner.

Japan's a
rich country.

Krakow's a
beautiful town.

75

Focus 2

Reading and listening

1 Which things can you see in the pictures?

> a servant   a housewife   a ship   a village
> the President of the United States
>
> ▶ Vocabulary book page 43.

2 **a)** Read the sentences about life in 1900. Which five sentences do you think are true?

b) Compare answers with a partner.

> I think number one is true.

> Mmm, I'm not sure …

3 ▭ [9.2] Listen and check.

In 1900 …

1 … there were only about 9,000 cars in the world. Today there are about 650 million.

2 … there weren't any telephones or radios.

3 … the journey from New York to Europe by ship was about six days.

4 … there were about one and a half million people in the world. Today there are about six billion.

5 … most women were housewives – or servants.

6 … there weren't any women at university.

7 … California and Florida weren't part of the USA.

8 … Vienna was a very important city in the world, but Hollywood was only a small village.

9 … Moscow wasn't the capital of Russia.

10 … Abraham Lincoln was President of the United States.

HAMBURG-AMERIKALINIE   ⅗ DEUTSCHLAND

was and *were*

4 **a)** Complete the sentences 1–6 below about 1900 with *was*, *were*, *wasn't* or *weren't*.

b) 📼 [9.3] Listen and check your answers.

Pronunciation

1 📼 [9.4] Listen and practise.

was /wəz/ … Victoria was Queen of England.

were /wə/ … Cars were very slow.

2 📼 [9.5] Listen and practise.

wasn't /wɒzənt/ … Driving wasn't safe.

weren't /wɜːnt/ … Roads weren't very good.

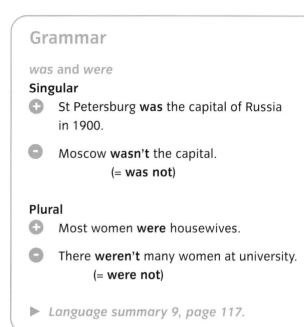

1 The President of the United States in 1900 .... William McKinley.

2 Queen Victoria .... the Queen of England, and Nicolas II .... the Tsar of Russia.

3 There .... many cars in the world, but bicycles .... very popular. In Britain, for example, there .... 600,000 bicycles in 1900!

4 Cars .... very slow. Roads .... very good, and driving .... always safe.

5 Coca-Cola .... a popular drink in America, but it .... well-known in other countries.

6 There .... a lot of trains, but there .... any aeroplanes. The first aeroplane .... in 1907.

Focus 3

Reading and vocabulary

1 Look at the pictures of Toru Mitsui and Estelle Dupont and read the captions.

a) Which countries are they from?

b) When were they born?

c) How old were they in 2000?

d) Were their families rich or poor?

2 **a)** Check the words in **bold**. Who do you think said these things about their childhood – Toru Mitsui or Estelle Dupont?

▶ Vocabulary book page 44.

a) 'Our home was very **comfortable**.'

b) 'My mother was always **ill**.'

c) 'My younger brother **died** when he was seven.'

d) 'I was very unhappy, it was a very **bad** time.'

e) 'Life was very **difficult**; sometimes we were **hungry**.'

f) 'Life is **better** now.'

b) Read and check.

Born in 1900

Toru Mitsui was 100 in 2000. He was born in a small village near Hiroshima in Japan. His parents were poor farmers. Today he lives with his son, Seiji, who is 76.

Estelle Dupont

was also 100 years old in 2000. She was born near Bordeaux in France, where her father was a rich businessman. Today she lives in an old people's home in Paris.

" Things were very different then. We were poor, and life was very difficult. Sometimes there wasn't much food, and sometimes we were hungry. There was no school in the village – we worked on the farm. There were eleven children in our family. My younger brother, Jun, was my best friend, but when he was seven he died. I was very sad. Our house was very small; there were six boys in one bedroom! But it's funny, we were usually happy ... my childhood was a happy time in my life. "

" My father was a rich businessman and we lived in a chateau about ten kilometres from Bordeaux. Our home was very comfortable. The house was very big – there were twenty bedrooms, beautiful gardens ... and lots of servants! But my childhood wasn't happy. I was an only child, and my mother was always ill. She died when I was eight, and my father died two years later when I was ten – it was a very bad time. I was a very unhappy child ... life is better now! "

3 Work in two groups. Group A reads about Toru Mitsui and Group B reads about Estelle Dupont. Answer the questions.

a) What was his/her father's job?

b) Where was his/her home?

c) Was his/her house small?

d) How many children were there in the family?

e) Was he/she happy?

Questions with *was* and *were*

> **Grammar**
>
> **Questions with *was* and *were***
>
> | | |
> |---|---|
> | **Was** she happy? | Yes, she **was**. |
> | | No, she **wasn't**. |
> | **Were** his parents rich? | Yes, they **were**. |
> | | No, they **weren't**. |
> | **Were** you happy? | Yes, I **was**. |
> | | No, I **wasn't**. |
>
> *Wh-* questions
>
> What **was** his job?   Where **were** they from?
>
> ▶ *Language summary 9, page 117.*

4 **a)** Practise the questions and answers from Exercise 3 with a partner from your group.

b) Work with a student from the other group. Student A asks about Estelle Dupont and Student B asks about Toru Mitsui.

5 **a)** Find four opposite pairs of adjectives.

> noisy   tall   short   good
> quiet   naughty   dirty   clean

b) Write questions using the prompts below.
Were you tall or short for your age?

When you were eight years old ...

– tall or short for your age?

– usually clean or dirty?

– a quiet child or a noisy child?

– nice to your brothers and sisters?

At school

– happy at school?   – good at maths?

– naughty?   – good at sport?

– your teacher nice?

Favourites

– What/your favourite game?

– What/favourite book or film?

– What/your favourite food?

– Who/your best friend?

Speaking task

1 Remember the time when you were eight years old. Think about your home, your family and your school.

2 Work in pairs. Interview your partner about his/her childhood.

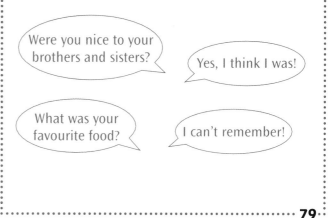

Were you nice to your brothers and sisters?

Yes, I think I was!

What was your favourite food?

I can't remember!

Real Life

Years and ages

1 🔲 [9.6] Listen and say these years.

1900	1950	1990	1995
1984	1999	2000	2002
2005			

▶ Vocabulary book page 45.

2 🔲 [9.7] Write down the years you hear.

a = 1995

3 a) When and where were these people born, do you think? Match the people with these years and places.

Chicago, USA, 1901
Skopje, the Balkans, 1910
Italy, 1935
New York, 1940
Louisville, USA, 1942
Hawaii, 1967
Somalia, 1955
Wales, 1969

b) 🔲 [9.8] Listen and check. Ask and answer questions with a partner.

When was Walt Disney born?

He was born in 19..

Where was he born?

He was born in ...

Walt Disney

Catherine Zeta-Jones

Mother Teresa

Luciano Pavarotti

Iman

Al Pacino

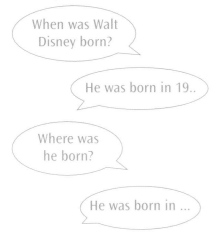
Nicole Kidman

Muhammad Ali

4 Ask three other students in your class.

Where were you born?

I was born in Rio de Janeiro.

And when were you born?

In 1980.

Speaking task

1 a) Write the answers to five of these questions on a piece of paper.

- Where were your brothers/sisters born?
- When were they born?
- Where was your mother born?
- When was she born?
- Where was your father born?
- When was he born?
- Where were your grandparents born?
- When were they born?

b) Write sentences. Do not write your name.

My brother was born in 1982. My grandmother was born in Mexico.

2 a) Give your papers to your teacher. Read your new sentences.

b) Ask questions to find whose paper you have.

Where was your mother born?

Do you remember?

▶ Language summary, page 117
▶ Vocabulary book, pages 42–46

1 a) Put *was* or *were* in the gaps.

a) ...Were........ you at school yesterday?

b) .... your grandfather a doctor?

c) .... you at home at 8.00 this morning?

d) .... your mother born in Europe?

e) .... you at work at 3.00 yesterday afternoon?

f) .... you born before 1980?

b) Ask and answer the questions with a partner.

2 Choose the correct answer.

a) I *was/were* in Germany a year ago.

b) Erika's mother *was/were* a famous actress.

c) We *wasn't/weren't* at home this morning.

d) I *wasn't/weren't* at work on Monday.

e) My friends *was/were* at the same school.

f) You *wasn't/weren't* here two weeks ago.

g) My grandfather *was/were* from Portugal.

3 a) Write the adjectives.

a) R O P O   p.oor........................

b) F A E S   s.............................

c) Y S U B   b.............................

d) G Y U L   u.............................

e) R O T H S   s.............................

f) L A N C E   c.............................

g) W O L S   s.............................

b) Write the opposites.

poor – rich

4 Match the years with how we say them.

1)	1964	a)	nineteen eighty-nine
2)	1998	b)	two thousand and thirteen
3)	2003	c)	nineteen forty-six
4)	1989	d)	nineteen ninety-eight
5)	2013	e)	two thousand and three
6)	1946	f)	nineteen sixty-four

module 10

Creative people

- ▶ **Grammar:** Past Simple affirmative; regular and irregular verbs
- ▶ **Vocabulary:** life events (start school, get married, etc.)
- ▶ **Real life:** months and dates

Coco Chanel –
French fashion designer
1883–1971

Charlie Chaplin – British
actor and director 1889–1977

Vincent van Gogh –
Dutch artist 1853–1890

Bob Marley – Jamaican singer
and musician 1945–1981

Focus 1

Past Simple: irregular verbs

1 Match sentences a–h with the people in the pictures.
▶ Vocabulary book page 47.

a) In 1886 he left Holland and went to live in France with his brother, Theo. *Vincent van Gogh*

b) She was from a poor French family, and when she was young she worked in a hat shop.

c) He made his first reggae album *Catch a Fire* in 1972.

d) In 1912 he left England and went to work in Hollywood.

e) She became a very rich and successful businesswoman.

f) He met his wife Rita at a concert, and then she became a singer in his band The Wailers.

g) He made over 100 films, and had four wives and twelve children!

h) He sold pictures in an art gallery in Holland before he became an artist.

2 ▭ [10.1] Listen and check your answers.

3 <u>Underline</u> the past tenses in a–h in Exercise 1.

In 1886 he left Holland and went to live in France with his brother, Theo.

Irregular past forms

Write the verbs for these irregular Past Simple forms.

...*leave*...... left

.... sold

.... went

.... met

.... wrote

.... became

.... made

.... had

▶ Vocabulary book page 63.

▶ *Language summary 10, page 117.*

4 ▭ [10.2] Listen and check. Practise saying the verbs and past tenses.

5 Complete sentences a–h with verbs in the Past Simple.

a) Chanel's clothes *became*. (become) popular in the 1920s.

b) Charlie Chaplin .... (make) his first film in 1914.

c) In 1952 Charlie Chaplin .... (leave) the USA, and .... (go) to live in Switzerland.

d) Bob Marley .... (have) a son, Ziggy Marley, who's also a reggae singer.

e) She also .... (make) perfume, especially the famous 'Chanel Number 5'.

f) Vincent Van Gogh .... (sell) only one painting in his life.

g) Bob Marley .... (meet) the Beatles at a concert in Los Angeles in 1975.

h) One of Chaplin's daughters, Geraldine, also .... (become) an actress.

6 a) Work in teams. Answer the quiz below. In some questions there is more than one answer.

b) ▭ [10.3] Listen and check your answers.

7 Use the names in the box (or your own ideas) to write sentences about **six** creative people.

Cervantes wrote Don Quixote.

> Agatha Christie   Cervantes   Greta Garbo   Leonardo Da Vinci
> Federico Fellini   Tolstoy   Gianni Versace   Adnan Saygun

Quiz

1 John Lennon:

a) sang with the Beatles.

b) wrote songs.

c) wrote detective stories.

2 Shakespeare wrote:

a) *Anna Karenina.*

b) *Don Quixote.*

c) *Romeo and Juliet.*

3 Billie Holiday:

a) made films.

b) sang blues and jazz.

c) sang reggae.

4 Elvis Presley:

a) was an actor.

b) was a singer.

c) wrote jazz.

5 Audrey Hepburn was:

a) an actress.

b) a writer.

c) a fashion designer.

6 Mozart wrote:

a) poetry.

b) jazz.

c) operas.

Focus 2

Reading

1 Look at the pictures below. Who is the boy and who is the woman?

2 Read about J. K. Rowling's life. Put these events in order.

a) ☐ She finished her first Harry Potter book.
b) ☐ She got married and had a daughter.
c) ☐ She studied French at university.
d) ☐ She became very famous.
e) ☐ She moved to Scotland.
f) ☐ She started writing her first Harry Potter book.
g) |1| She wrote her first story, *Rabbit*.
h) ☐ She worked in Portugal as an English teacher.
i) ☐ She was unemployed.

3 ▭ [10.4] Listen and read to check your answers.

Past Simple: regular verbs

Grammar

Past Simple: regular verbs

| work | + ed | work**ed** |
| start | + ed | start**ed** |

look!

| live | + d | live**d** |
| study | → ied | stud**ied** |

▶ *Language summary 10, page 117.*

The Writer and the Wizard

J.K. Rowling was born in England in 1965. She loved reading, and wrote her first story, 'Rabbit', when she was only six years old. She studied French at university, then worked as a secretary in London. She had the idea for Harry Potter when she was on a train. 'Harry just walked into my head,' she said later. She started writing the first Harry Potter book the next day.

In 1992 she went to live in Portugal for three years. She wrote Harry Potter in the morning, and worked as an English teacher in the afternoon and evening. She got married to a Portuguese TV journalist and had a daughter called Jessica.

Then she returned to Britain and lived in Edinburgh, in Scotland. She was unemployed at that time, and wrote in cafés because they were warmer than her small flat. After five years she finished the first book, 'Harry Potter and the Philosopher's Stone'. The book sold millions of copies all over the world, and Joanne Kathleen Rowling became very famous. She is now very rich, but she still writes her books in cafés!

4 Write the past forms of these regular verbs.

a) watch b) work c) start

d) like e) talk f) return

g) love h) hate i) marry

▶ Vocabulary book page 48.

Pronunciation

1 🔲 [10.5] Listen to the past forms. Which have two syllables?

2 Listen again and practise the verbs.

---

5 Complete the sentences about J. K. Rowling. (Some verbs are irregular.)

a) As a child, she .... (like) reading. She .... (write) her first story when she .... (be) six.

b) After university, she .... (work) as a secretary.

c) She .... (have) the idea for Harry Potter on a train journey, and .... (start) writing the book the next day.

d) In Portugal, she .... (work) as a teacher in the afternoon and evening, and .... (write) Harry Potter in the morning.

e) In Edinburgh, she .... (live) in a small, cold flat.

f) She .... (finish) the first Harry Potter book in a café.

6 Tick (✓) the things that have happened in your life. Check the past forms of the verbs.

▶ Vocabulary book pages 62–63.

- [ ] – born in ...... (town)
- [ ] – brother/sister born
- [ ] – start school
- [ ] – leave school
- [ ] – meet ...... (a good friend)
- [ ] – move house
- [ ] – change schools
- [ ] – start university
- [ ] – leave university
- [ ] – start work
- [ ] – meet ..... (your partner)
- [ ] – get married
- [ ] – change jobs
- [ ] – have a son/daughter

Speaking task

1 Draw a time line for your life, like this. Write the things that have happened to you on the line.

1979 My brother was born.

1982 I started school.

1976 I was born in Milan.

1988 We moved house.
1989

1993   1995

2 Work in pairs. Tell your partner about your life line.

I was born in Milan in 1976 and in 1979 my brother was born ...

Focus 3

Reading and vocabulary

1 You are going to read the Legend of King Arthur.
Was Arthur:

– a Welsh King? – a Scottish King? – an English King?

2 Find these things in the pictures.

> a magic sword   a castle   a soldier   a knight
> a lady   an arm   a wizard   a battle
> ▶ Vocabulary book page 49.

3 Read the text. Match the names (1–6) with the explanations (a–f).

1	Camelot	a)	where Arthur sat with his knights
2	Sir Lancelot	b)	Arthur's sword
3	Excalibur	c)	Arthur's castle
4	Guinevere	d)	a wizard, Arthur's teacher and friend
5	Merlin	e)	Arthur's wife
6	The Round Table	f)	Arthur's best friend

Listening

4 ▭ [10.6] Listen and read again.

5 **a)** Make sentences from the story.
   ▶ Vocabulary book pages 62–63.

Arthur was born in Tintagel Castle.

1	Arthur (be born)	a)	in a terrible battle.
2	He (become)	b)	king when he was fifteen.
3	The Lady of the Lake (give)	c)	in Tintagel Castle.
4	King Arthur (live)	d)	Guinevere.
5	He (marry)	e)	a magic sword to Arthur.
6	But Guinevere (love)	f)	at Camelot, with his knights.
7	Arthur (die)	g)	Sir Lancelot.

b) Compare answers with a partner.

6 Are there any legends about famous Kings in your country? What are the Kings' names? What happened in the story?

King Arthur was born at the Castle of Tintagel, in England. His parents weren't married, so the baby boy went to live with Merlin, a wizard.

With the help of Excalibur, Arthur became a good soldier and a great King.

(b)

Merlin became Arthur's friend and teacher. He taught Arthur everything he needed to know to become King.

(c)

One day, when Arthur was fifteen, he went out with Merlin. They were near a lake when they saw the white arm of a lady in the water. In her hand there was a magic sword, Excalibur. The Lady of the Lake gave the sword to Arthur. Everyone knew then that he was their next King.

(e)

He lived in the castle of Camelot, where there was a famous Round Table. There Arthur and his knights sat to talk about their battles.

(f)

Arthur married the beautiful Guinevere, but she loved Sir Lancelot, one of Arthur's knights and his best friend.

(g)

One day, in a terrible battle, Arthur told one of his men to throw Excalibur back into the lake, and the hand of the Lady of the Lake took back the sword. Excalibur disappeared forever. Arthur died in battle.

Venice Carnival: February 1st–12th

Day of the Dead, Mexico: November 2nd

Independence Day, USA: July 4th

Real life

Months and dates

1 **a)** ☐ [10.7] Put these months in the correct place. Listen and check.

> January   March   May
> July   September   November
>
> ▶ Vocabulary book page 50.

|
― ....
― February
― ....
― April
― ....
― June
― ....
― August
― ....
― October
― ....
― December

b) Listen again and mark the stress. Practise saying the months.

Jȧnuary

2 **a)** Match these dates with the words.

1st — fourth
2nd — second
3rd — thirteenth
4th — twenty-first
10th — third
13th — first
21st — thirtieth
30th — tenth

b) ☐ [10.8] Listen and check.

3 ☐ [10.9] Listen and ⟨circle⟩ the date you hear.

a) ⟨21st⟩/31st   d) December 13th/30th
b) April 5th/15th   e) January 6th/16th
c) October 9th/19th   f) March 12th/20th

Seville Spring Fair:
April 16th–24th

Grammar

Dates

we write	we say …
March 17th	

March the seventeenth.

July 24th

July the twenty-fourth.

Look:

I was born **on** December 30th.
I was born **in** December.

4 Find a student with a birthday close to yours.

When's your birthday?

March 5th.

My birthday's on March 8th!

5 Look at the photographs above. Write four dates like these that are important in your country.

Do you remember?

► Language summary, page 117
► Vocabulary book, pages 47–51

1 Find six regular verbs and seven irregular verbs.

O	S	T	U	D	Y	M	S
F	B	O	N	G	I	A	L
I	A	D	W	O	R	K	H
N	Z	G	S	E	E	E	A
I	M	E	E	T	T	J	V
S	U	T	M	E	U	L	E
H	S	E	L	L	R	I	L
I	K	N	A	W	N	V	X
V	W	A	T	C	H	E	P

2 Write the Past Simple of the verbs in Exercise 1.

3 Choose the correct answer.
a) Joao *met*/*started* Veronica in 1992.
b) Carla and Roberto *got*/*became* married on May 19th.
c) We *moved*/*changed* house in March.
d) Vanessa *left*/*changed* jobs two months ago.
e) Agatha Christie *made*/*wrote* seventy-nine books in her life.
f) My wife and I *had*/*was born* our first son in 2001.

4 **a)** Put these dates in order.

July 22nd	☐	June 4th	☐
January 1st	☐	September 30th	☐
October 2nd	☐	December 25th	☐
February 14th	☐	August 3rd	☐
March 1st	☐	April 16th	☐
November 21st	☐	May 1st	☐

b) Work with a partner. You say a date from Exercise 4a). Your partner says the day before.

July 22nd.   July 21st.

module 11
Going away

- ▶ **Grammar:** Past Simple: negatives and questions; *and* and *but*
- ▶ **Vocabulary:** irregular verbs; holiday expressions
- ▶ **Real life:** buying a train ticket

in the country

a town near the sea

a big city

Focus 1

Vocabulary: holidays

1 Look at pictures a–c. Which is the best place to go on holiday?

2 What can you do in these places? Compare answers in pairs.

> go to the beach   go to museums   go skiing
> go for a walk   go shopping   go to restaurants
> stay in a hotel   go swimming
>
> ▶ Vocabulary book page 52.

In a big city you can go to museums.

3 **a)** Write the names of three popular places in your country.

a) a big city

b) a place in the country/ in the mountains

c) a town near the sea/ a lake/a river

b) Tell your partner what people usually do in these places.

In Bodrum, people usually go to the beach.

In Bariloche, people go skiing or go for walks.

90

Past Simple negative

> ### Grammar
>
> **Past Simple negative**
> We **didn't go** to expensive restaurants.
>   (= **did not**)
> *I/you/he/she/they* are the same.
> They **didn't have** a lot of money.
> I **didn't see** you last week.
>
> ▶ *Language summary 11A, page 118.*

6 **a)** Write sentences about Matt and Claire's holiday. Use the information in Exercise 5.

a) They went for a walk in Manhattan.
b) (go shopping)
c) (go to the Metropolitan Museum)
d) (go to the Statue of Liberty)
e) (go to the Empire State Building)
f) (stay in a hotel)
g) (stay with friends)
h) (go for a walk in Central Park)

b) ▭ [11.2] Listen and check.

7 **a)** Make correct sentences about your day yesterday.

1 I got up late. ✓
2 I had eggs for breakfast.
   I didn't have eggs for breakfast.
   I had toast and coffee.
3 I went to work.
4 I had a big lunch.
5 I went to the cinema.
6 I watched TV in the morning.
7 I wrote an email to a friend.
8 I had dinner at home.
9 I went to bed early.

b) Compare your sentences with another student.

> I didn't get up late, I got up at seven o'clock. What about you?

> I got up very late, at quarter past eleven!

Listening

4 **a)** Look at the pictures of New York. Think of three places you can visit there.

b) ▭ [11.1] Listen to Matt talking about his holiday in New York. Did he enjoy it?

5 Listen again. Tick (✓) the things Matt and Claire did in New York, and cross (✗) the things they didn't do.

a) [✓] go for a walk in Manhattan
b) [ ] go shopping
c) [ ] go to the Metropolitan Museum
d) [ ] go to the Statue of Liberty
e) [ ] go to the Empire State Building
f) [ ] stay in a hotel
g) [ ] stay with friends
h) [ ] go for a walk in Central Park
i) [ ] go to expensive restaurants

Focus 2

Vocabulary and speaking: holidays

1 Put the holiday vocabulary into **A – ways to travel,** or **B – things to do.**

> go by train **A**   go to nice restaurants   go by car   go by boat
> go to museums   go by plane   go shopping   relax and do nothing
> go to the mountains   go to the beach   go by bus
>
> ▶ Vocabulary book page 53.

2 When you go on holiday:

- which is your favourite way to travel?
- which don't you like?
- which things in Exercise 1B do you like doing?

3 Work in pairs. Ask and answer the questions about 'a holiday you remember well'. Write your partner's answers.

Past Simple questions

> ### Grammar
>
> **Questions**
> **Did** you **have** a good time?
>
> Where **did** you **go**?
> What **did** you **do**?
>
> **Short answers**
> Yes, I **did**.
> No, I **didn't**.
>
> ▶ *Language summary 11B, page 118.*

4 **a)** Put these questions in the correct order.

1 have/a/Did/holiday/nice/you ?
 Did you have a nice holiday?
2 do/did/you/last Sunday/What ?
3 go out/you/last night/Did ?
4 nice weekend/a/you/have/Did ?
5 watch TV/last night/you/Did ?

b) 🔊 [11.3] Listen and check. Practise saying the questions.

c) Choose three questions to ask your partner.

A holiday I remember well

⭐1 Where did you go? ....

⭐2 When did you go there?
a) this year
b) last year
c) .... years ago

⭐3 Did you travel ...
a) by car?
b) by plane or boat?
c) by train or bus?

⭐4 Where did you stay?
a) in a hotel
b) with family
c) with friends
d) other ....

⭐5 Did you go ...
a) with your family?
b) with friends?
c) alone?

⭐6 What did you do there?
a) go to the beach
b) go shopping
c) go for walks
d) other ....

⭐7 Did you have a good time?
a) Yes, I did.
b) No, I didn't.
c) It was okay.

5 a) Put the time words in order on the line.

yesterday   ~~last year~~   ~~this morning~~
last weekend   last night   last month

past ——————————————→ **now**
last
year .... this
morning

b) 🖭 [11.4] Listen and check. Practise saying the time words.

6 Use the prompts in the game below to make questions.

Example:

Did you get up early this morning?
What time did you get up?

Speaking task

Work in groups of three or four. Play the board game. (See page 112 for rules.)

Don't forget!

It's your turn.

Is it my turn?

… is the winner.

START ⭐	– get up early this morning? (What time?)	– go out last Saturday night? (Where?)	**rest** — have breakfast this morning? (What?)
go back to the start	– go shopping last weekend?	– phone any friends yesterday? (Who?)	**rest** — do any sport last weekend? (What?)
– speak English yesterday?	**rest**	– come to school by car today?	– see any films last weekend? (What?) **go back to the start**
– arrive early for this lesson?	– listen to any music yesterday? (What?)	**go to finish**	– sleep well last night? — read the newspaper yesterday? (Which?)
– read in bed last night? (What?)	**go to finish**	– cook dinner last night? (What?)	**rest** **FINISH** ⭐

93

Focus 3

Reading: Around the World

1 Do you like travelling by boat? When was the last time you travelled by boat? Where did you go? Did you enjoy it?

2 a) Look at the pictures and the title. What is the article about, do you think?

▶ Vocabulary book page 54.

a) It's about three brothers and three sisters who sailed around the world.

b) It's about six people in the same family who sailed around the world.

c) It's about two people who sailed around the world with their three children.

b) 📼 [11.5] Listen and read the text. Check your answers.

3 Correct the mistakes in these sentences. Compare answers in pairs.

a) Alison is an engineer and Jeff is a teacher.

b) They met at a golf club.

c) Their dream was to sail across the Atlantic.

d) They took their four children with them.

e) Their boat, the *Charlotte Rose*, was eighteen metres long.

f) They went to South America first, then Australia, and then South Africa.

g) Alison didn't enjoy the journey.

h) One day the children saw five whales near their boat.

i) Jeff says that the family argued all the time.

The family who sailed around the world

Engineer Jeff Dent, 46, and wife Alison, 44, always loved sailing. They first met at a sailing club and their dream was to sail around the world.

So, when Jeff became unemployed in January 1999, they decided to make their dream come true. Alison left her job as a teacher and they bought an eight-metre sailing boat, the *Charlotte Rose*. They wanted to sail from Britain to South Africa, then to Australia, across the South Pacific to Argentina, and back to Britain across the Atlantic.

They weren't the first people to make this journey, but this time there was one big difference – Jeff and Alison took their three children with them: ten-year-old Oliver, Charlotte, who was seven, and three-year-old Daniel.

Yesterday, after two years and 48,000 kilometres, they arrived back in Britain. To their surprise, hundreds of friends and journalists were there to meet them.

So how was it? "It was very difficult," said Alison, "but it was also the best two years of my life." The children also loved it. "We saw things that most people never see," said Oliver. "One morning we got up and there were three whales near the boat ... that was fantastic!"

There was one question everyone wanted to ask. Did they argue a lot? Jeff answered. "Of course we argued sometimes, but we were a great team. It was an amazing journey."

4 a) Find the past tenses of these verbs in the article, and write them in the box.

▶ Vocabulary book pages 62–63.

meet	..met..
decide	....
buy	....
want	....
take	....
arrive	....
see	....
argue	....

b) 🔲 [11.6] Listen and check. Which verbs are irregular?

5 For you, which of these words and phrases describe the Dents' journey? Compare answers with other students.

– dangerous   – exciting   – interesting   – boring
– a great idea   – a stupid idea

6 Discuss these questions with other students.

– Would you like to make a journey like the Dents'?

– Which places in the world would you like to visit? Why?

Grammar

and and *but*

Alison left her job as a teacher **and** they bought a sailing boat.
We argued sometimes **but** we were a real team.

---

7 Look again at the text and ⟨circle⟩ every *and* and *but*.

8 Join these sentences with *and* or *but*.

a) Tom's married. He has two children.
Tom's married and he has two children.
b) They went to Rome. They didn't go to Venice.
c) Marta went to Thailand on holiday. She had a great time.
d) I like English. I don't understand everything.
e) This is a good hotel. The rooms are very quiet.
f) Sue had a ticket for a concert. She didn't go.
g) I can play the guitar. I can't sing.

9 Complete these sentences for you. Compare your sentences with another student.

1 At the weekend I usually ....
   and ....
2 I like .... but I don't like ....
3 Last week I .... and ....
4 I can .... but I can't ....
5 I always .... but I never ....
6 Yesterday I .... and ....

Real life

Buying a train ticket

1 Match these words with the pictures below.

> train   a single (ticket)   a return (ticket)
> a platform   a ticket office
>
> ▶ Vocabulary book page 55.

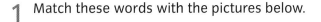

2 a) 🖭 [11.7] Listen to the conversation and circle the correct word.

VERONICA: Can I have a *single/return* to Oxford, please?

TICKET SELLER: OK, that's *£23.50/£25.30*.

VERONICA: Here you are. What time's the *last/next* train?

TICKET SELLER: Well, there's one at *10.54/10.24*.

VERONICA: Oh, good. Which *train/platform*?

TICKET SELLER: Platform *six/sixteen*.

VERONICA: OK, thanks a lot. Bye.

b) Practise the conversation with a partner. Close your books and try to remember the conversation.

3 Work in pairs – A and B.

Student A

1 You want to buy tickets to these places on the next train. Ask Student B questions to complete the table below. Imagine the time now is 11 a.m.

	price	time	platform
1 a return to Manchester	....	....	....
2 a single to Oxford	....	....	....

2 Turn to page 112 and answer Student B's questions.

Student B

1 Turn to page 110 and answer Student A's questions.

2 You want to buy tickets to these places on the next train. Ask Student A questions to complete the table below. Imagine the time now is 11 a.m.

	price	time	platform
1 a single to Liverpool	....	....	....
2 a return to Leeds	....	....	....

Do you remember?

▶ Language summary, page 118
▶ Vocabulary book, pages 52–56

1 a) Tick (✓) the sentences that are true for you. Make the other sentences negative.

     didn't play
a) I ~~played~~ tennis last month.

b) I went to the cinema last week.

c) I had a dog when I was a child.

d) My parents got married in 1975.

e) I went on holiday two years ago.

f) I met some friends at the weekend.

g) My mother lived in the country when she was young.

b) Compare your answers in pairs.

2 Put the words in the sentences.

     did
a) When ∧ he go to bed last night? (did)

b) Did come to school by train? (he)

c) What did they last night? (do)

d) What did you get up this morning? (time)

e) your sister go shopping last week? (did)

f) Where did you your husband? (meet)

3 Match answers 1–6 with questions a–f in Exercise 2.

1) At half past seven.

2) Yes, she did.

3) I met him on holiday.

4) No, he didn't.

5) At about eleven o'clock. a

6) They went to a concert.

4 Match the words and phrases in the box with the verbs.

a restaurant	with a family	shopping
a good time	swimming	the beach
breakfast	a museum	in a hotel
a lot of money	with friends	skiing

GO TO   GO

HAVE   STAY

module 12
Spending money

- ▶ **Grammar:** *want to*; *going to*
- ▶ **Vocabulary:** things you buy (furniture, clothes, etc.); colours and sizes
- ▶ **Real life:** social language

Focus 1

Vocabulary: things you buy

1 **a)** Which things can you see in each advert?

▶ Vocabulary book page 57.

① a carpet   a book   coffee   a magazine

② jeans   a jacket   a watch   boots

③ clothes   make-up   shampoo   a mobile phone

b) 🔲 [12.1] Practise saying the new words.

2 What is each advert for? Talk to a partner. Check on page 109.

I think this is an advert for a book.

It's for coffee, I think.

3 Which words in Exercise 1 go in these groups?
a) Things you carry with you – a mobile phone
b) Things you wear
c) Things in the house

(3)

6 Which of these things do you want to buy? Tell other students.

- clothes
- CDs or books
- furniture
- other things

I want to buy the new Radiohead CD.

I want a new handbag.

7 a) Write six **true** sentences about yourself from A, B and C.

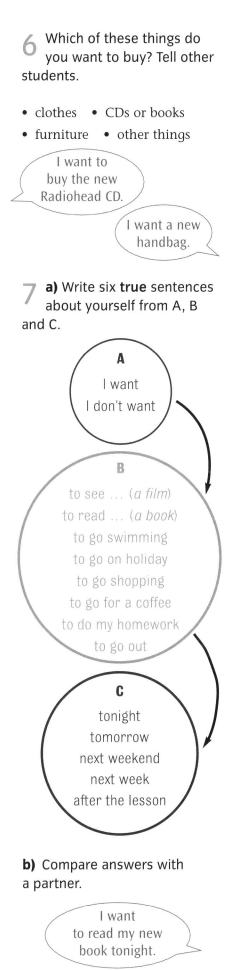

A
I want
I don't want

B
to see ... (*a film*)
to read ... (*a book*)
to go swimming
to go on holiday
to go shopping
to go for a coffee
to do my homework
to go out

C
tonight
tomorrow
next weekend
next week
after the lesson

b) Compare answers with a partner.

I want to read my new book tonight.

---

4 🔊 [12.2] Add these words to the correct group in Exercise 3. Listen and check.

> a jumper   a chair   a table   a lamp   shoes
> a handbag   a T-shirt   a briefcase
>
> ▶ Vocabulary book page 57.

want to

5 🔊 [12.3] Listen and write what four students want to buy.

a) Yuko ....

b) Antonia ....

c) Ali ....

d) Lucas ....

> ### Grammar
>
> *want* + noun
> I want **a CD.**
> I want a lamp.
>
> *want* + *to* + verb
> I want **to buy** a CD.
> I **don't want** (to buy) anything.
>
> ▶ *Language summary 12A, page 118.*

Focus 2

Vocabulary: colours and sizes

1 Match the words to the colours (a–g) below.

> black   blue   brown   red
> green   yellow   white
>
> ▶ Vocabulary book page 58.

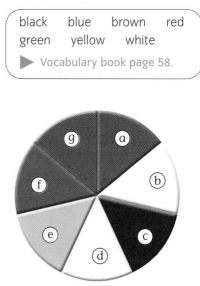

2 **a)** Match answers a–c with questions 1–3.

1 What colour is it?

2 How much is it?

3 What size is it?

a) small/medium/large/size 38

b) $125/£60

c) yellow/red/black

b) 🖭 [12.4] Listen and check. Practise the questions and answers.

Reading

3 Look at the two Internet shopping sites. What can you see in the pictures?

4 Look at 'extra information' on page 101. Which pictures do they describe?

Extra information:

classicblackleather.com

BL307 Short leather jacket, made in Italy.

Men's sizes medium/large/extra large $195

Women's sizes small/medium/large $175

Children's sizes ages 5–6 years/7–8 years $85

(boys/girls) ages 9–10 years/11–12 years $105

colours: black only

BL201 Quality leather briefcase, made in Brazil.

Suitable for men or women.

medium (38cm x 25cm) $85

large (44cm x 32cm) $95

colours: black/brown

Extra information:

worldcrafts.com

EI 33A Pure wool jumper for men and women.

Colours:
brown and white/black and white/
blue and white

sizes:

extra small/small $45
medium/large/extra large $58

EI 67C Handmade coffee table from South India.

Large: 70cm x 45cm x 30cm high $130

Small: 45cm x 45cm x 30cm high $85

---

5 Work with a partner. You have three minutes to answer as many questions as you can.

1 What sizes are the men's jackets?
2 Is there a medium size coffee table?
3 How much is a large jumper?
4 Where is the briefcase from?
5 Can you buy the jumper in yellow?
6 How much is a jacket for a ten-year-old child?
7 Which is cheaper, the men's jacket or the women's jacket?
8 What colours are the briefcases?
9 Who is the jumper for – men, women or both?
10 How many centimetres high are the two coffee tables?

Speaking task

1 Choose a present from the pictures for:

a) a man you know
(your father/husband/a friend)
b) a woman you know
c) your teacher
d) a child you know
e) yourself

Think about what each person likes.

2 Work in small groups. Tell the other students what you want to buy and who it is for.

For my brother, I want to buy the leather jacket.

What size?

Don't forget!

For my sister, I want to buy … (*a jumper*).

What colour?
What size?

One o'clock on Saturday afternoon.

Focus 3

going to

1 Look at the shopping mall. What places do you see?

2 Look at the people numbered 1–7. Which people are these sentences about?

▶ Vocabulary book page 59.

a) **6** She's going to buy some flowers.
b) ☐ They're going to have lunch.
c) ☐ She's going to play tennis.
d) ☐ They're going to watch a football match this afternoon.
e) ☐ Perhaps he's going to buy a new computer.
f) ☐ They're going to go home.
g) ☐ He's going to meet his girlfriend.

3 **a)** ▭ [12.5] Listen to four of the people. Who is talking?

a – number 6

b) ▭ [12.6] Can you complete the sentences? Listen and check.

1 My mother's in hospital so I'm .... visit her this afternoon.

2 We're .... visit the Castle Museum. Then we' .... find a hotel.

3 I'm .... going to buy a computer today.

4 I'm .... meet my girlfriend's parents this evening. We' .... have dinner at their house.

102

Grammar

going to

I and *you* forms

➕ I'm **going to visit** my mother in hospital.

➖ I'm **not going to buy** a computer today.

❓ What **are** you **going to do**?

he/she/we/they forms

He/She**'s** going to play tennis.

We**'re** going to visit the museum.

They**'re** going to watch a football match.

▶ *Language summary 12B and C, page 118.*

4 Ask and answer questions about the people in the picture.

What's she going to do?

She's going to buy some flowers, then she's going to visit her mother in hospital.

5 ▭ [12.7] Match questions 1–6 with answers a–f. Listen and check.

1 Are you going to phone Linda today?
2 Are you going to drive to the airport tomorrow?
3 Are you going to go out tonight?
4 Are you going to go to the shops this morning?
5 Are you going to have a holiday this year?
6 What are you going to do when you finish university?

a) No, I'm going to watch that Woody Allen film on TV … I'm really tired.
b) Yes, soon. Do you want something?
c) Yes, I think we're going to stay with my aunt and uncle in London.
d) No, she's going to phone me.
e) I don't know. I think I'm going to work with my father.
f) I'm going to take the bus, I think.

Pronunciation

1 ▭ [12.8] Listen and notice that *to* is weak in these sentences.

　　　　　　/tə/
Are you going to phone Linda today?

　　　　　　/tə/
Are you going to go out tonight?

　　　　　/tə/
No. I'm going to watch TV.

2 Practise the conversations in Exercise 5.

Speaking task

1 You are going to ask other students about next weekend. First, write down the questions that you are going to ask.

Are you going to visit friends next weekend?

Find one person in the class who …

1 is going to visit friends.
2 is going to meet a friend.
3 is going to do some sport.
4 is going to work or study.
5 is going to buy some new clothes.
6 is going to go to another town.
7 is going to see a film or concert.
8 is going to sleep a lot.

2 Ask different students the questions. Write the name of the one person in each box above.

3 Tell the class.

Oscar's going to visit friends next weekend.

Real life

Best wishes for the future

1 Match the phrases in the box with pictures a–e.

> Have a nice weekend!   Have a nice holiday!
> See you in September!
> Good luck with your new job!
> Good luck with your new school!
>
> ▶ Vocabulary book page 60.

2 **a)** 🔲 [12.9] Listen and check. Repeat the conversations.

b) Practise the conversations with a partner.

ⓒ

Anna is going to start a
new school soon.

ⓐ

Lisa is going to start
a new job soon.

ⓓ

Tristan is going to go on
holiday next week.

ⓑ

Mike is going to Paris
next weekend.

ⓔ

It is the end of your English course
this year. You are going to start the
next course in September.

Do you remember?

3 a) Make similar phrases using the prompts below.

1 Have a nice … !

> day time evening
> meal birthday

2 Good luck with your … !

> new car test
> job interview

3 See you … !

> in January on Monday
> at seven o'clock next week

b) 🖭 [12.10] Listen and check. Practise the phrases.

4 What do you say to your partner in these situations?

1 It is your partner's birthday tomorrow.

2 Your partner is going to go to a very nice restaurant for dinner this evening.

3 Your partner is going to move to a new flat next weekend.

4 Your partner is going to go to Italy on holiday next week.

5 You are going to meet your partner for coffee at three o'clock this afternoon.

5 Tell other students about something you are going to do soon.

> I'm going to buy a new motorbike this weekend.

> Good luck!

► Language summary, page 118
► Vocabulary book, pages 57–61

1 Find three words for each group and write them in the table below.

O	K	J	S	H	O	E	S	K	R
J	N	U	K	M	S	I	J	B	P
E	U	M	C	T	S	H	I	R	T
A	P	P	I	I	H	D	E	I	O
N	S	E	D	M	A	R	G	E	G
S	G	R	E	E	N	E	N	F	B
A	B	O	N	U	D	K	I	C	L
T	A	B	L	E	B	N	M	A	U
M	P	R	A	E	A	A	F	S	E
X	O	G	M	W	G	W	R	E	D
C	A	R	P	E	T	E	S	R	A

clothes	
colours	
things in the house	
things made of leather	shoes

2 Tick (✔) the things that are true for you. Make the other sentences negative. Compare your answers.

a) I'm ∧not going to be a doctor.

b) I'm going to study English next year.

c) I want to live for 100 years.

d) I'm going to go out tomorrow evening.

e) I want to be famous.

f) I'm going to have a holiday next month.

g I want extra homework today.

3 Put the sentences in order.

a) tomorrow/I/going to/'m/football/play/not

I'm not going to play football tomorrow.

b) a new car/'s/going to/My sister/buy

c) their friend/going to/'re/They/in hospital/visit

d) going to/not/next year/I/go to university/'m

e) me/going to/meet/'s/Marta/at the airport

f) next weekend/with my parents/stay/'re/going to/We

Consolidation
modules 9–12

A Grammar and speaking: Past Simple

1 Put the verbs in brackets in the Past Simple.

When I was young I lived in Scotland, in a village near the sea. Life (a) ..was.. (be) very different then. It was the 1930s, so there wasn't any TV, but my family (b) .... (have) a radio, and we (c) .... (listen) to it every evening. My parents (d) .... (have – negative) a car, so I (e) .... (go) to school by bicycle – six miles every day! But I (f) .... (study – negative) very hard, and (g) .... (leave) school when I was fourteen.

There (h) .... (be – negative) any cinemas near our village, so every Saturday I (i) .... (meet) my friends on the beach and we (j) .... (play) football all day. When I was fifteen my parents (k) .... (sell) our house and the family (l) .... (move) to England. I never went back to my village, but I can still hear the sea in my head ...

2 ▭ [1] Listen and check your answers.

3 Think about your life when you were a child and make notes on these topics.

> home   school   your free time   friends
> holidays   games and sports
> things you liked (food, books, films ...)

4 Work in groups of three or four. Tell the other students about your life when you were a child.

B Grammar: quiz

Work in teams. <u>Underline</u> the correct words. There's one point for each correct answer.

(a) When *did/was/ were* you born?

In/On/At November 28th, 1924.

(b) Did Pablo *start/started/starts* his new job last week?

No, he *did/was/ were* ill.

(c) What *want you/ you do want/do you want* to do after you leave school?

I want *that I go/to go/ go* to university.

(d) Where *went you/ did you go/did you went* last weekend?

I went to Paris *on/ by/with* train.

(e) What *you going/ you are going/are you going* to do tonight?

I/I'm/I can going to watch TV.

(f) *Were/Did/Was* your parents rich?

No, they *didn't/ wasn't/weren't*.

C Speaking: *yes/no* questions

1 Write these things in the boxes below. Don't write the answers in order.

- something you're going to do next weekend.
- a person you talked to on the phone last week.
- something you want to buy.
- a person you want to meet.
- a place you went to last month.
- something you can do well.
- a place you want to visit.
- a person you're going to see tomorrow.
- something you like doing in your free time.

2 Swap books with another student. Ask questions to find out why he/she wrote the things in the boxes.

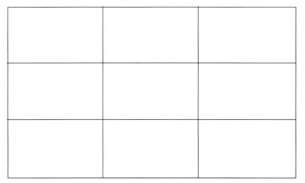

D Pronunciation: sentence stress

1 🔲 [2] Listen and mark the stressed words in these sentences.

a) Where were you born?
b) He wasn't very old.
c) I went to a museum at the weekend.
d) She didn't come to school.
e) What are you going to do?
f) I'm going to meet my friends.

2 Listen again and check. Practise saying the sentences.

E Song – *Money, Money, Money*

1 Match the money words.

a) wealthy   1) a bill
b) rich   2) man
c) win   3) a fortune
d) pay   4) man

2 🔲 [3] Listen to the song. Complete the gaps in the chorus with the words in the box.

had   world   things   rich
always   man's   funny

£££££££££££££££££££££££££££

Chorus

Money, money, money,
Must be .... ,
In the .... man's world.
Money, money, money,
.... sunny,
In the rich .... world.
Aha-ahaaa
All the .... I could do
if I .... a little money.
It's a rich man's ....

£££££££££££££££££££££££££££

3 Listen to the song again. Put the verses in the correct order.

$$$$$$$$$$$$$$$$$$$$$$$$$$$$

a) ☐ And still there never seems to be a single penny left for me.
b) ☐ In my dreams I have a plan,
c) ☐ I wouldn't have to work at all, I'd fool around and have a ball.
d) ☐ If I got me a wealthy man,
e) ☐1☐ I work all night, I work all day, to pay the bills I have to pay.
f) ☐ Ain't it sad?
g) ☐ That's too bad.

Chorus

h) ☐ So I must leave, I'll have to go,
i) ☐8☐ A man like that is hard to find but I can't get him off my mind.
j) ☐ And win a fortune in a game – my life will never be the same.
k) ☐ And if he happens to be free I bet he wouldn't fancy me.
l) ☐ To Las Vegas or Monaco.
m) ☐ Ain't it sad?
n) ☐ That's too bad.

Repeat Chorus x 2

$$$$$$$$$$$$$$$$$$$$$$$$$$$$

Communication
activities

Module 1: Focus 4, Exercise 4, page 12.

Student A

BINGO

2	11	14	8
12	20	5	17
7	15	4	19
8	17	18	9

Module 5: Real life, Exercise 4, page 46.

Student A

Roleplay 1

You are a customer.

You want to buy these things:

- five postcards
- a phone card (£5)
- a TV magazine
- stamps

Useful language

Do you have a/any ... ?

How much are they?

Can I have a/some/five ... ?

Thanks a lot.

Roleplay 2

You are a shopkeeper.

You have these things in your shop:

Useful language

Do you have a/any ... ?

We only have ...

That's five pounds/twenty p ...

Anything else?

That's three fifty, please.

Module 6: Focus 3, Reading and Vocabulary, Exercise 8, page 53.

The real couples are:

Isabel and Antony

Melanie and Oliver

Grant and Nicole

Module 8: Real life, Exercise 4b), page 71.

The answers to the quiz are:

1b)   2c)   3c)   4b)   5b)   6b)   7a)

Module 12: Focus 1, Vocabulary, Exercise 2 page 98.

Advert 1 is for carpets.

Take A Closer Look At Allied Carpets

Allied CARPETS

Advert 2 is for boots.

Russell&Bromley FOOTWEAR

D800

For high flyers everywhere

www.sendo.com

Advert 3 is for a mobile phone.

sendō

Module 5: Real life, Exercise 4, page 46.

Student B

Roleplay 1

You are a shopkeeper.

You have these things in your shop:

Useful language

We (only) have ...

That's five pounds/thirty p ...

Anything else?

That's three fifty, please.

Roleplay 2

You are a customer.

You want to buy these things:

- a newspaper in your language
- tissues
- three stamps
- a computer magazine

Useful language

Do you have a/any ...?

How much are they?

Can I have a/some/ten ...?

Thanks a lot.

Module 11: Real life, Exercise 3, page 96.

Student B

Oxford	Manchester
single – £12.60	single – £37.20
return – £15.30	return – £48.50
Trains leave at:	**Trains leave at:**
10.30, 10.48, 11.18	10.15, 10.45, 11.45
Platform 7	Platform 13

Module 1: Focus 4, Exercise 4, page 12.

Student B

Module 7: Real life, Exercise 4, page 63.

Student B

Ask your partner what time the programmes start, and write the times.

What time does *Holiday* start?

Twenty-five past eight.

Module 7: Real life, Exercise 4, page 63.

BBC 1

7.50	House and Garden
....	Holiday!
10.00	The BBC News
....	Dracula

BBC 2

....	The Simpsons
7.55	Sports World
....	The X Files
10.30	Newsnight

ITV

7.50	Star Wars
....	The Doctors
10.00	ITV Evening News
....	Elton John in concert

CHANNEL 4

....	Channel Four News
7.55	Go Shopping!
....	Friends
9.10	The Day Today

Module 4: Speaking task, page 33.

Don't forget!

"In my picture there's a (*café*)."

"Yes, in my picture too."

"There are two (*buses*) in my picture."

"There's a (*big tree*) on the left of the (*café*)."

Picture B

Module 3: Speaking task, page 29.

Sun and Moon café

Food

cheese sandwich	£2.20
egg sandwich	£1.90
burger	£3.20
cheeseburger	£4.60
pizza	£5.20
salad	£3.95
chips	£1.50

Drinks

Coke	£1.00
bottle of water	£1.20
coffee	£1.30

Module 11: Real life, Exercise 3, page 96.

Student A

Liverpool	**Leeds**
single – £32.60	single – £44.90
return – £44.60	return – £57.70
Trains leave at:	**Trains leave at:**
10.35, 11.30, 11.55	10.50, 11.15, 11.45
Platform 16	Platform 3

Module 7: Focus 3, page 60.

Mostly a: You don't make the best of your free time because you don't really have any free time! You are very hardworking, but remember: everybody needs to relax sometimes!

Mostly b: Your life is well-balanced: you work hard, but you also make the best of your free time.

Mostly c: You really enjoy your free time, but do you have any time for work or studying? Don't burn the candle at both ends!

Module 1: Focus 4, Exercise 4, page 12.

Student C

BINGO

14	7	19	9
6	10	8	3
9	2	12	13
20	17	7	5

Module 11: Speaking task, page 93.

Rules for board game

1   Play with a dice and counters/coins. The first player (player 1) throws the dice and lands on a square.

2   He/She uses the word prompts on that square to ask a question to the person on his/her left (player 2). If player 2 answers correctly it is his/her turn. If he/she does not, the question is asked to the next player on his/her left (player 3) and so on. Player 2 then misses his/her turn.

3   If player 1 lands on a 'rest' square or a 'go back to start' square, player 2 automatically has the next turn.

4   The winner is the first player to reach the 'finish' square.

Language summary

Module 1

A Personal pronouns and possessive adjectives

personal pronouns			possessive adjectives	
I	*I'm Rosa. I'm a doctor.*	my	*My name's Peter.*
you	*Are you Andy?* *Are you a student?*	your	*What's your name?* *What's your job?*
he	*He's a footballer.*	his	*What's his name?* *His name's Tony.*
she	*She's a singer.*	her	*Her name's Jennifer.* *What's her job?*

> **REMEMBER**
> *I/you/he/she* + **verb**
> *my/your/his/her* + **noun**

B *a* and *an* with jobs

a + consonant (b, c, d, f …)	*an* + vowel (a, e, i, o, u)
I'm a teacher. *I'm a businessman.* **NOT** ~~I'm businessman.~~	*I'm an actor.* *She's an engineer.* **NOT** ~~She's engineer.~~

Module 2

be: I/you/he/she/it

⊕ Positive

I'm (= I am)	*I'm from Spain.*
you're (= You are)	*You're Italian.*
he's (= he is)	*He's a student.*
she's (= She is)	*She's twenty-three.*
it's (= It is not)	*It's in London.*

⊖ Negative

I'm not (= am not)	*I'm not from Spain.*
You're not or You aren't (= are not)	*You're not French.* *You aren't a doctor.*
he isn't (= is not)	*He isn't from Russia.*
she isn't (= is not)	*She isn't fifty.*
it isn't (= is not)	*It isn't in Washington.*

❓ Questions

am I … ?	*Am I late?*
are you …?	*Where are you from?*
is he … ?	*Is he French?*
is she … ?	*Where's she from?*
is it … ?	*Is it a big city?*

Question words

What	's	your/his/her	name? job?
Where	are	you	from?
	's	he/she/it	
How old	are	you?	
	is	he/she/it?	

Module 3

Ⓐ *be: we/you/they*

<table>
<tr><td colspan="2">➕ Positive</td><td colspan="2">➖ Negative</td><td colspan="2">❓ Questions</td></tr>
<tr>
<td>we're
(= We are)</td><td>We're on holiday.</td>
<td>we're not (= are
not) or We aren't</td><td>We aren't
very happy.</td>
<td>Are we ...?</td><td>Are we in
London?</td>
</tr>
<tr>
<td>you're
(= You are)</td><td>You're Italian.</td>
<td>you're not
or You aren't</td><td>You're not
French.</td>
<td>Are you ...?</td><td>How are
you?</td>
</tr>
<tr>
<td>they're
(= They are)</td><td>They're at the
beach.</td>
<td>they're not
or They aren't</td><td>They aren't
in the hotel.</td>
<td>Are they ...?</td><td>Where are
they from?</td>
</tr>
</table>

Ⓑ Singular and plural nouns Ⓒ *this, that, these, those*

singular	plural
a hotel	hotels
a student	students
a bus	buses
a city	cities
a man	men
a woman	women
a child	children
a person	people

Module 4

Ⓐ *there is, there are*

<table>
<tr><td></td><td>singular</td><td>plural</td></tr>
<tr><td>➕</td><td>There's a car park near the station.</td><td>There are three cafés.
There are some hotels.</td></tr>
<tr><td>➖</td><td>There isn't a cinema in our town.</td><td>There aren't any restaurants.</td></tr>
<tr><td>❓</td><td>Is there a post office in this street?</td><td>Are there any shops here?</td></tr>
</table>

Ⓑ *some* and *any*

- We use *some* in **positive** sentences. → There are **some** shops.
- We use *any* in **negative** sentences. → There aren't **any** people.
- We also use *any* in **questions**. → Are there **any** shops?

Ⓒ Prepositions of place

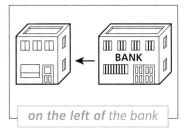

on the left of the bank

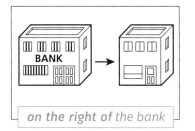

on the right of the bank

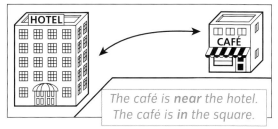

*The café is **near** the hotel.*
*The café is **in** the square.*

Module 5

A Possessive 's

Laura is Tony's wife.
~~Laura is the wife of Tony.~~
Rosa is Carlos and Carmen's daughter.

> **REMEMBER**
> *Laura's a student.*   **'s** = is
> *Carlos is Laura's father.*   **'s** = possessive

C yes/no questions

do	subject	verb	...
Do	you	**study**	English?
Do	they	**live**	in a flat?
Short answers			

Do you live in England?
*Yes, I **do**.*   *No, I **don't**.*
~~Yes, I live.~~   *~~No, I don't live.~~*

B Present Simple: *I, you, we* and *they*

+ Positive	− Negative (*don't* + verb)
*I **live** in France.*	*I **don't study** French.*
*You **work** with computers.*	*You **don't have** any brothers.*
*We **have** an expensive car.*	*We **don't work** for a big company.*
*They **study** three languages.*	*They **don't live** in the country.*

D *Wh-* questions

question word	do	subject	verb	...
Where	do	you	live?	
What	do	they	study	at school?
Who	do	you	live	with?

Module 6

A Present Simple: *he* and *she*

+ Positive	− Negative (*doesn't* + verb)
Bill lives in the USA. *He likes football a lot.*	*He doesn't like cooking.* *Tom doesn't live in Italy.* **NOT:** ~~doesn't lives~~
She reads a lot of books. *Rita works with children.*	*She doesn't read books.* *Ana doesn't use a computer.* **NOT:** ~~doesn't uses~~

B Spelling: verbs with *he* and *she*

Most verbs: add *-s*
work → work**s**   live → live**s**
Verbs ending in *-ch, -sh* **or** *-o:* **add** *-es*
watch → watch**es**   go → go**es**
Verbs that end in *-y:* *-y* → *-ies*
study → stud**ies**
Irregular form:
have → **has**

C yes/no questions: *he* and *she*

does	subject	verb	...
Does	he	**like**	cats?
Does	she	**eat**	meat?
Short answers			

Yes, he/she does. No, he/she doesn't.
~~Yes she likes.~~

D Subject and object pronouns

subject pronouns (*before* the verb)	object pronouns (*after* the verb)
I love Italian food.	My wife loves **me**.
You don't understand.	Nice to meet **you**.
He/She works in New York.	He/She doesn't like **him/her**.
It's a very nice city.	I don't like **it**.
We don't live here.	He talks to **us**.
You're English.	Where are **you**?
They watch TV a lot.	I don't know **them**.

Module 7

A Adverbs of frequency

never   not usually   sometimes   usually   always

0%   100%

B Present Simple: word order

subject	adverb	verb	...
I	always	get up	early.
Pedro	usually	has	coffee for breakfast.
My brother	sometimes	plays	football at the weekend.
Children in Britain	don't usually	go	to school on Saturday.
Japanese people	never	wear	shoes in the house.

C Time expressions

on	in	at
on Monday **on** Thursday afternoon	**in** the morning **in** the afternoon **in** the evening	**at** half past five **at** ten o'clock **at** the weekend **at** night

> REMEMBER
>
> *every* + day, week, month, year, morning, afternoon, evening, night, Monday, Tuesday, Wednesday ...

D *Wh-* questions with *he* and *she*

Question word	*does*	subject	verb	...
Where	does	he	work?	
What	does	she	study	at school?
Who	does	Isobel	live	with?

Module 8

A *can* and *can't*

+ Positive   **− Negative**   **? Questions**   **Short answers**

I You He She We They	**can** swim well. **can** play the guitar.	I You He She We They	**can't** read music. **can't** speak French. (= **cannot**)	Can you cook? Can he play chess? Can she drive? Can they swim?	Yes, I can. Yes, he can. Yes, she can. Yes, they can.	No, I can't. No, he can't. No, she can't. No, they can't.	

B Question words

Who ...?	asks about a **PERSON**
What ...?	asks about a **THING**
When ...?	asks about a **TIME**
Where ...?	asks about a **PLACE**
Why ...?	asks about a **REASON**
How many ...?	asks about a **NUMBER**

Who	is		your teacher?
What	does	he	do at work?
When	do	you	watch TV?
Where	does	she	live?
Why	are	you	late?
How many people	are	there	in your class?

Module 9

Past Simple of *be*

	➕ Positive	➖ Negative	❓ Questions
singular	I **was** very sad.	I **wasn't** very happy. (= **was not**)	**Was I** late?
	You **were** rich.	You **weren't** poor. (= **were not**)	Where **were you** born?
	He **was** a teacher.	He **wasn't** a doctor.	Who **was he?**
	She **was** short.	She **wasn't** very tall.	**Was she** born in the USA?
	It **was** an expensive car.	It **wasn't** a cheap car.	What **was it?**
plural	We **were** at home.	We **weren't** at school.	When **were we** in Italy?
	You **were** at the cinema.	You **weren't** at the theatre.	**Were you** unhappy?
	They **were** French.	They **weren't** Italian.	Where **were they** from?

Short answers to *yes/no* questions

Were you a happy child?	Yes, I **was.**/No, I **wasn't.**
Was he/she/it very old?	Yes, he/she/it **was.** No, he/she/it **wasn't.**
Were his parents rich?	Yes, they **were.** No they **weren't.**

> **REMEMBER**
> You can also use *was* and *were* with *there:*
> **There was** a large park.
> **There weren't** any good restaurants.
> How many people **were there**?

Module 10

Past Simple – positive sentences

regular verbs
Most regular verbs: add *-ed* start → start**ed** work → work**ed** return → return**ed** Verbs ending in *-e*: add *-d* live → live**d** hate → hate**d** Verbs ending in *-y*: change *-y* to *-ied* study → stud**ied**

irregular verbs
Many common verbs are irregular: go → **went** have → **had** write → **wrote** make → **made** Sorry, there are no rules for irregular verbs! Look at the **Verb table** on page 63 of the **Vocabulary book** for a list of common irregular verbs.

> **REMEMBER**
> a The Past Simple is the **same** for *I, you, he, she, it, we* and *they.*
>
> b We sometimes use these words and phrases with the Past Simple:
> • **yesterday**
> • **(two years) ago**
> • **last night/week/month**

Module 11

Ⓐ Past Simple negative

subject	*didn't*	verb	...
I	didn't (= did not)	study	English last year.
He/She	didn't	go	to work.
They	didn't	stay	in a hotel.

REMEMBER

Present Simple	Past Simple
I **don't** like football.	I **didn't** like football.
He **doesn't** get up late.	He **didn't** get up late.
Where **do** you live?	Where **did** you live?
When **does** he start work?	When **did** he start work?

Ⓑ Past Simple questions

question word	*did*	subject	verb	...
Where	**did**	you	**go**	on holiday?
When	**did**	he	**leave**	university?
What	**did**	they	**do**	last night?
	Did	you	**watch**	TV last night?
	Did	she	**go**	on holiday last year?

Short answers

Did you go by train? Yes, I **did**. ~~Yes, I went.~~
No, I **didn't**. ~~No, I didn't go.~~

REMEMBER

You don't use *did* in negatives or questions with *was* and *were*.
~~He didn't was rich.~~   ~~Did they were from Turkey?~~

Module 12

Ⓐ want

want + noun

➕ I **want** a mobile phone.

➖ She **doesn't want** any furniture.

❓ **Do** you **want** some new shoes?

want to + verb

➕ We **want to** go to the beach.

➖ He **doesn't want to** watch TV.

❓ **Does** she **want to** go swimming?

REMEMBER

We sometimes use these words and phrases with *going to*:
- **this afternoon/evening**
- **tonight**
- **tomorrow**
- **next week/weekend/month/year**

Ⓑ *going to* – positive sentences

subject + *be*	*going to*	verb	...
I'm	going to	meet	my friends tomorrow.
You're	going to	do	your homework.
He's/She's	going to	play	tennis this afternoon.
We're	going to	see	a film tonight.
They're	going to	get	married next month.

Ⓒ *going to* – negative and question forms

➖ Negative

subject + *be*	*not going to*	verb	...
I'm/We're	not going to	come	to class tomorrow.
He's/She's/ They're	not going to	watch	the match on TV.

❓ Question

question word	*be*	subject	*going to*	verb	...
What	are	they	going to	do	this evening?
	Are	you	going to	ask	him tonight?

Tapescripts

Module 1

Recording 3

a) A: What's your name, please?
    B: Abdul Hussein.
b) C: Hi, I'm Martina. What's your name?
    D: My name's Vanessa.
c) E: Hello, are you Mr Bellini?
    F: Yes, that's right.
d) G: Hello, my name's Peter Gregory.
    H: Hi, I'm Andrea Martin. Nice to meet you.
e) I: Are you Mrs Adams?
    J: No, I'm Mrs Davis.

Recording 4

a) businessman, businesswoman
b) actor
c) police officer
d) student
e) engineer
f) waiter
g) doctor
h) teacher

Recording 5

1   Hi, my name's Marie Suchel and I'm a doctor.
2   Hello, I'm Philip Morgan and I'm an actor.
3   I'm a police officer. My name's Louise Dent.
4   Hello, my name's Tibor Molnar and I'm an engineer.
5   I'm a businesswoman. My name's Kristina Johanssen.
6   Hi, my name's Olivier. I'm a waiter.

Recording 6

a) I'm a waiter.   b) I'm an actor.   c) I'm an engineer.
d) I'm a businesswoman.

Recording 7

a) Her name's Jennifer Lopez. She's a singer and an actress.
b) His name's Tony Blair. He's a politician.
c) Her name's Serena Williams. She's a tennis player.
d) His name's Luis Figo. He's a footballer.

Recording 8

A: What's his name?
B: His name's Luis Figo.
A: What's his job?
B: He's a footballer.
A: What's her name?
B: Her name's Jennifer Lopez.
A: What's her job?
B: She's a singer.

Recording 10

a b __ d __ f __ h __ j __ l m n __ p
__ __ s t u __ __ x __ z

Recording 11

a) How do you spell 'actor'?
b) How do you spell 'politician'?
c) How do you spell 'engineer'?
d) How do you spell 'teacher'?
e) How do you spell 'businessman'?
f) How do you spell your surname?
g) How do you spell your first name?
h) How do you spell your teacher's surname?

Recording 12

a) What's your surname?
b) And what's your first name?
c) What's your full name, please?
d) And how do you spell that, please?

Recording 13

a) A: Paula, this is Antonia.
    B: Hi, Antonia. Nice to meet you.
    C: Nice to meet you!
b) C: Hello, Steve!
    D: Hello, how are you?
    C: Fine, thank you. And you?
    D: I'm very well, thanks.
c) E: Goodbye!
    F: Bye Kris, See you later.
    G: Yes, see you!

Recording 16

a) Look at your teacher.   g) Close your book.
b) Open your book.   h) Say your name.
c) Look at page seven.   i) Write your name.
d) Look at the picture.   j) Work with a partner.
e) Look at page ten.   k) Say 'hello'.
f) Read your book.

Module 2

Recording 1

1 the USA   2 Brazil   3 Great Britain   4 France   5 Spain   6 Italy
7 Poland   8 Turkey   9 Russia   10 Japan

Recording 3

A: Where are you from?
B: I'm from São Paulo, in Brazil. And you?
A: I'm from Russia.
B: Are you from Moscow?
A: No, I'm not from Moscow. I'm from St Petersburg.
B: Are you a student?
A: Yes, I'm at St Petersburg University.

Recording 4

1   The Blue Mosque's in Istanbul, in Turkey.
2   Leonardo DiCaprio isn't British or Italian. He's American.
3   Anna Kournikova isn't an actress or a singer. She's a tennis player.
4   Rivaldo is from Brazil.
5   Sony isn't an American company or a British company, it's a Japanese company.
6   A Ferrari is an Italian car.

Recording 6

a) Hello, my name's Claudia, and I'm from Venice, in Italy.
b) Hi, my name's Mike. I'm from Melbourne, in Australia.

c) Hello, I'm Lamai, and I'm from Bangkok, in Thailand.
d) I'm from Cairo, in Egypt, and my name's Mohammed.
e) I'm Belen, and I'm from Barcelona, in Spain.
f) I'm Franz, and I'm from Hamburg, in Germany.

Recording 8

twenty, twenty-one, twenty-two, twenty-three, twenty-four, twenty-five, twenty-six, twenty-seven, twenty-eight, twenty-nine

Recording 9

a) seventy-five b) forty-four c) thirty-six d) fifty-two
e) sixty-eight f) ninety-one g) twenty h) eighty-seven

Recording 10

a) She's fifteen. b) She's thirty-three. c) He's ninety-two.
d) He's forty-eight. e) He's twenty-two. f) She's fifty-nine.
g) He's forty-seven. h) He's two.

Recording 11

Part A
Teacher: These are two of my friends. This is my friend Nikos. He's from Greece. From Athens. He's a waiter, and he's twenty-six years old.
Part B
T: This is my other friend. You ask me questions, okay?
Student 1: What's her name?
T: Her name's Judit.
S: Jud..it. How do you spell that?
T: J-U-D-I-T.
S1: Thank you.
S2: Where's she from?
T: She's from Budapest.
S2 Budapest?
T: Yes, Budapest ... in Hungary.
S2: Oh yes, Hungary ... okay.
T: More questions ...
S3: What's her job?
T: She's a teacher at Budapest University.
S3: A teacher?
T: Yes, she's an English teacher!
S3: Oh, okay.
S4: And how old is she?
T: She's twenty-seven. No, twenty-eight. She's twenty-eight.
S4: Twenty-eight?
T: Yes!

Recording 13

C = clerk; R = Rita
C: Hello.
R: Hi.
C: Please sit down.
R: Thanks.
C: So first of all, what's your first name?
R: Rita.
C: That's R-I-T-A?
R: That's right, yes.
C: And your surname?
R: Kirmani.
C: How do you spell that?
R: K-I-R-M-A-N-I.
C: K-I-R-M-A-N-I. Fine ... okay, Rita, and are you married?
R: Yes, I am.
C: And how old are you?
R: Er, I'm thirty-two.
C: Okay. And what's your address, please?
R: It's 87, Sangley Road ...
C: How do you spell that?
R: S-A-N-G-L-E-Y

C: 87 Sangley Road...
R: London ... SE6 1BH.
C: ... SE6 1BH. That's fine. And what's your home phone number?
R: 020 8695 2441.
C: 020 8695 2441 ... and what's your work number?
R: 020 7322 8424.
C: 7322 8424 ... okay, thank you. And what's your job, please?
R: I'm a teacher.
C: A teacher. Right ... and you say you're interested in applying for ...

Recording 14

a) What's your surname?
b) What's your first name?
c) Are you married?
d) How old are you?
e) What's your address?
f) What's your phone number?
g) What's your job?

Module 3

Recording 2

A: Paris and Madrid are capital cities.
B: Warsaw is in Poland.
A: Egypt and Oman are hot countries.
B: São Paulo and Rio de Janeiro are Brazilian cities.
A: Ferraris are expensive cars.
B: Scotland is a cold country.
A: Sydney and Melbourne are in Australia.

Recording 3

1 They're from Brazil.
2 We aren't students.
3 They aren't married.
4 We're on holiday.

Recording 4

a)
We're from Beirut in Lebanon, and we're in London on holiday. We are staying with friends from Lebanon, and we're very happy here. London is beautiful, but the weather isn't very good!
b)
I'm from Milan, and Emre's from Ankara in Turkey. We aren't on holiday, we are students at London University. London is fantastic for students, but it's very expensive!
c)
We're from St Petersburg in Russia. We are doctors and we're in London for a conference. The conference is very good, but we aren't very happy with our hotel. It's very expensive and the rooms are very small.

Recording 5

Food: bread, meat, rice, pasta, fish, fruit, eggs, vegetables, cheese
Drink: coffee, milk, water

Recording 6

a) A: Dad, what's this?
    B: It's cheese, Sam.
b) C: Look at that old car!
    D: Yes, it's beautiful.
c) E: Are these bananas?
    F: Yes, they're red bananas.
d) G: Those shoes are nice.
    H: Yes, they are.

Recording 7

a) Look! What's that building?
b) Who are those children?
c) These postcards, please.
d) Tomas, this is Vanessa. Vanessa, this is Tomas.

Recording 8

a) twelve dollars fifty
b) four euros
c) six twenty-five
d) forty-five p
e) fifty-nine ninety-nine
f) three pounds seventy
g) seven ninety

Recording 10

a) A: Yes, please?
   B: A burger and chips, please.
   A: Sure. Anything else?
   B: No, thanks.
b) C: Three coffees, please.
   D: Here you are.
   C: Thank you.
c) E: How much is that?
   F: Five ninety, please.

Recording 11

W = Waitress J = Jake S = Sue P = Paul
W: Hi, are you ready to order?
J: Yes, I think we are ... Sue?
S: Er, a burger ... and ... a salad, please.
W: Okay, ... and for you, sir?
P: A pizza for me, please.
W: So that's a a burger, a salad ... and a pizza.
J: And can I have a burger and chips, please?
W: Okay. Any drinks?
S: A coke, please.
P: Just water for me.
W: And for you?
J: Oh, er ... a coke for me, too.
W: So that's two cokes and a bottle of water.
J: That's right.
W: Anything else?
P: No, that's all, thanks.
W: Okay, thanks a lot.

Module 4

Recording 1

1 a café   2 a bus stop   3 a restaurant   4 a post office   5 a hotel
6 a station   7 a bank   8 a park   9 a car park   10 a cinema
11 a supermarket

Recording 2

A Okay, there's a square ... and in the square there's a café with some people in it ... there's a woman with her baby ... and also a group of three young women. And there are two waiters in the café and er, what else? On the left of the café there's a restaurant, and on the right there's a hotel. There's a dog in the square, and some children ... five children, two boys and three girls, and there are lots of trees in the square, and near the trees there are two old women.

B Okay, there's a square ... and in the square there's a café with some people in it ... there's a man with his baby ... and also a group of three young women. And there is one waiter in the café and er, what else? On the left of the café there's a hotel, and on the right there's a supermarket. There are two dogs in the square, and some children ... three children, three boys and one girl, and there is one tree in the square, and near the tree there are two old men.

Recording 6

a) A: Is this Eden Street?
   B: Sorry, I don't know.
b) C: ¿Dónde está la farmacia?
   D: Sorry, I don't understand.
c) E: Sorry!
   F: That's okay.
d) G: Excuse me, where's the station?
   H: It's over there, on the right.

Consolidation modules 1–4, recording 1

a) A: What's your name?
   B: Julia Maria Campos.
b) A: Where are you from?
   B: I'm from Cartajena, in Colombia.
c) A: What's your job?
   B: I'm an engineer.
d) A: How old are you?
   B: I'm thirty-six.
e) A: Are you married?
   B: No, I'm single.
f) A: What's your address?
   B: Avenida San Martin No 9-159.
g) A: What's your phone number?
   B: 575 665 7433
h) A: Is there a university in your city?
   B: Yes, there is.

Consolidation modules 1–4, recording 2

Hello, Goodbye
You say yes, I say no.
You say stop and I say go go go. Oh no.

You say goodbye and I say hello
Hello hello.
I don't know why you say goodbye, I say hello
Hello hello.
I don't know why you say goodbye, I say hello.

I say high, you say low.
You say why and I say I don't know. Oh no.
You say goodbye and I say hello
(Hello Goodbye Hello Goodbye) hello hello
(Hello Goodbye) I don't know why you say goodbye, I say hello
(Hello Goodbye Hello Goodbye) hello hello
(Hello Goodbye) I don't know why you say goodbye
(Hello Goodbye) I say goodbye.

Why why why why why why do you say goodbye goodbye, oh no?

You say goodbye and I say hello
Hello hello.
I don't know why you say goodbye, I say hello
Hello hello.
I don't know why you say goodbye, I say hello.

You say yes (I say "yes") I say no (but I may mean no.)
You say stop (I can stay) and I say go go go (till it's time to go oh), oh no.

You say goodbye and I say hello
Hello hello.
I don't know why you say goodbye, I say hello
Hello hello.
I don't know why you say goodbye, I say goodbye
Hello hello.
I don't know why you say goodbye, I say hello hello...

Module 5

Recording 2

a) Laura is Marta's mother.
b) Tony is Carmen's son.
c) Laura is Tony's wife.
d) Carlos and Carmen are Rosa's parents.
e) Luis is Marta's brother.
f) Carlos and Carmen are Luis's grandparents.
g) Marta and Luis are Tony and Laura's children.

Recording 5

Louise
I don't have any brothers or sisters.
I work for a big company.
Gabor
I have a one-year-old daughter.
I don't have a job.
I study a lot.
Carolina
I work in a school.
We have a big garden.
I don't live in a flat.

Recording 9

Maggie's possessions: passport, glasses, money, purse, CD
Richard's possessions: credit card, watch, magazine, camera
Ellen's possessions: radio, mobile phone, wallet

Recording 10

S = Sally A = Andy
S: Excuse me.
A: Yes?
S: Hi, my name's Sally. I work for Phillips and Jones, a market research company. Do you have a few minutes to answer some questions?
A: Er ... yeah, sure.
S: Thanks. Okay, first, how old are you?
A: I'm twenty-four.
S: Okay ... And do you have a job?
A: Yes, I work for a travel company.
S: And you're male ...
A: Yes!
S: Right. Do you have a computer?
A: Yes, I do.
S: And how about a PlayStation?
A: No, not now ...
S: Okay. And a TV? Do you have a television?
A: Yes ... three!
S: Three! And so do you have a video too?
A: Yes, I like TV!
S: And a DVD player?
A: No, not yet.
S: And what about music? Do you have a CD player?
A: Yes, in my bedroom.
S: And what about a mobile phone ... do you have a mobile phone?
A: No, I don't. I don't like them!

S: Okay. Do you have a camera?
A: Yes, a very nice one, actually.
S: And the last question. Do you have any credit cards?
A: Yes, two; Visa and Mastercard.
S: Okay. Thanks very much.
A: No problem. Bye.
S: Bye.

Recording 11

S = Silvia N = Newsagent
S: Do you have any Italian newspapers?
N: No, sorry. We only have English newspapers.
S: Oh, OK. How much are the phone cards?
N: They're five pounds.
S: Er ... can I have two? And these postcards, please.
N: Sure. That's ... er ... £11.50, please.
S: Thanks. Do you have any stamps?
N: No, but there's a post office in the High Street.
S: OK, thanks a lot. Bye.
N: Goodbye.

Module 6

Recording 2

a) A: Do you like dancing?
   B: Yes, I love it.
b) A: Do you like cats?
   B: No, I hate them.
c) A: Do you like rock music?
   B: It's okay.
d) A: Do you like Tom Cruise?
   B: Yes, I like him a lot.
e) A: Do you like Julia Roberts?
   B: No, I hate her!
f) A: Do you like reading in English?
   B: Yes, I love it!

Recording 3

E = Emma S = Simon
E: Right, the first one. 'Most men don't like cooking.' Mmm, yes, I think that's true, definitely.
S: Mmm, I'm not sure. I hate it, but I think some men like cooking ... When they have time ....
E: Hmmm ... I think most men like eating, not cooking!
S: Okay, the next one ... most children don't like school, yes, that's true, for sure!
E: No, I don't think it's true ... some children don't like school, but a lot of children really like school ... my children love school!
S: ... right ... and the next one ... most children watch TV every day ... yes, I think that's true, in America anyway. My son watches a lot of TV ...
E: Yeah, it's true in England too. My children watch TV after school. But what about this one ... 'most men don't like shopping'. Is that true, do you think?
S: No, I don't think so. I like shopping, and all my friends like shopping, I think ...
E: Yeah, my husband likes shopping too ... so it's not true! And this one, most women don't play computer games .... I don't know ... I don't play computer games, but I don't know about other women ... what about your friends?
S: Erm ... I don't know .... my sister plays computer games a lot, she really likes them, but I don't know about her friends
E: OK, so we're not sure about that one ...
S: And the last one, 'most old people don't use the Internet' ... Well, in the USA lots of old people use the Internet, so I don't think that's true. What do you think?
E: Well my father uses the Internet all the time, yeah, and he's

seventy-six! And he emails his friends every day. So I don't think that's true ...

Recording 4

a) My children love school.
b) My son watches a lot of TV.
c) My husband likes shopping too.
d) My sister plays computer games a lot.
e) My father uses the Internet all the time.

Recording 6

1 A: Does Melanie like dancing?
   B: Yes, she does.
2 A: Does Isabel eat meat?
   B: No, she doesn't
3 A: Does Nicole like music?
   B: We don't know.

Recording 7

four o'clock   quarter past four   half past four   quarter to five

Recording 8

a) seven o'clock
b) ten o'clock
c) twelve o'clock
d) half past six
e) quarter past six

f) quarter to seven
g) quarter to nine
h) quarter past nine
i) half past one
j) half past twelve.

Recording 9

a) The train now leaving platform 8 is the seven o'clock to Manchester Piccadilly. Passengers for the seven o'clock train to Manchester Piccadilly, please go to platform eight.
b) A: See you later then.
   B: Okay, see you at quarter past eight in front of the cinema, yeah?
   A: Yeah, bye.
c) It is now quarter to six. The store is closing in fifteen minutes. I repeat, the store is closing in fifteen minutes.
d) A: Excuse me, can you tell me the time?
   B: Yeah, it's half past three.
   A: Thanks.

Module 7

Recording 1

1 get up   2 have breakfast   3 go to work   4 start work
5 have lunch   6 finish work   7 get home   8 have dinner
9 go to bed   10 sleep

Recording 3

My daily routine ... well ... I get up at about ten o'clock, and I usually have breakfast in the garden ... if it's a nice day. I love sitting in the garden reading the newspaper. I have lunch at about two, and then practise my violin in the afternoon. Concerts in Liverpool usually start at eight, so I leave home at half past six and get the train to the city centre. After the concert ... er ... well ... I finish work at about half past ten, then have dinner in a restaurant with some friends from the orchestra. I usually take a taxi from the restaurant, and get home at about half past twelve. Then I watch TV or read a book, and go to bed at about two o'clock in the morning. And that's my day.

Recording 4

1) Monday   2) Tuesday   3) Wednesday   4) Thursday   5) Friday
6) Saturday   7) Sunday

Recording 5

A: Monday, Tuesday
B: Thursday, Friday
A: Sunday, Monday
B: Saturday, Sunday
A: Wednesday, Thursday
B: Tuesday, Wednesday
A: Friday, Saturday
B: Sunday, Saturday

Recording 6

A Yes, In Dubai ... people sometimes have tea with their breakfast, but usually they drink coffee ... or milk.
People never wear shoes in the house ... no we don't wear shoes in the house.
This one ... yes we usually have a big lunch ... and yes, we usually sleep in the afternoon ... it's very hot here in the afternoon!
We don't usually have dinner at 10.00 ... that's very late for us in Dubai ... we usually eat at about 7.00 or 8.00.

B Yes, we sometimes have tea with our breakfast, but usually we have coffee ... or hot chocolate ... children usually have hot chocolate with their breakfast.
Yes, in France, we usually have a big lunch ... we like our lunch! But no, we don't usually sleep in the afternoon.
Yes, of course we always kiss our friends when we meet ... or if it is two men, they shake hands usually.
No, we don't usually have dinner at 10.00. We start dinner at 8.00 usually, but sometimes we stay at the table until 10.00!

Recording 7

meet friends   go to the cinema   read a book
do your homework   stay in   watch TV   listen to music
clean the house

Recording 9

a) A: What's the time?
   B: Er ... it's twenty past four.
   A: Thanks.
b) ... and in Cinema World today there's an interview with the Hollywood actor Arnold Schwarzenegger. That's at ten past two, after the news and weather ...
c) A: Excuse me, have you got the time?
   B: Yes, of course. It's ... er ... five to ten.
   A: Thanks very much.
d) A: Hi, Sally.
   B: Hi. Do you want to see that new film tonight?
   A: Yeah, sure. What time does it start?
   B: Er ... let me see. It starts at twenty-five to eight, but I think we need to go there a bit ...
e) A: What time do you usually get up?
   B: About twenty past six.
   A: Oh, you get up before me, I usually ...
f) A: What time is the football on tonight?
   B: Mmmm. Well, it starts at twenty-five past nine, but there's a good film on the other side.
g) Teacher: Mario, what's the time?
   Mario: Er ... it's ten to three.
   Teacher: Time for a break then, I think.

Tapescripts

Recording 10

L = Louise G = Greg

L: What's on TV tonight?

G: Let me see ... well, there's The News, that starts at seven o'clock. Or on the other side there's George Michael in Concert.

L: What time does that start?

G: Er, ten past seven.

L: Hmmm ... What else? Are there any good films on?

G: Well, there's *Titanic*, that starts at ten to eight.

L: What, again?!

G: ... or there's *Casablanca*. You know, that classic movie with Humphrey Bogart. It starts at ... er ... let's see ... five to nine.

L: What's on Channel 4?

G: Not much ... oh, there's Football Night ...

L: What time?

G: Er ... Half past nine.

L: Mmm ... I know, let's go to the cinema. There's that new Will Smith film on in town, and ...

Module 8

Recording 2

a) She can't cook very well.

b) We can play chess.

c) He can speak Chinese.

d) My parents can't speak English.

e) My grandmother can't swim very well.

Recording 3

B = Ben K = Karis

B: Okay ... mmm, so let's think ... can you drive?

K: Yes, you know I can! How about you?

B: Yes, of course!

K: Okay, can you ride a bicycle then?

B: Erm, no I can't actually ... I don't like bicycles very much ... can you?

K: Yes, I ride my bicycle to work every day.

B: Mm ... okay ... what next ... can you swim a hundred metres?

K: Mmm yes I think I can ... I'm not very good at swimming, but ... yes, I can swim a hundred metres, I think ... can you?

B: Yes ... I'm a very good swimmer! Mm, what else? I know, languages ... which languages can you speak?

K: French ... a little bit ...

B: Aha! But can you speak Spanish?

K: No ... why? Can you?

B: Yes I speak very good Spanish ...

K: Mmm ... What about music! Can you play the violin?

B: No, I can't ... of course I can't! You know I'm not musical! Can you play the violin?

K: Yes, I was in the school orchestra! I was very good! So that's two to me!

B: Okay ... mmm ... this is difficult ... what else? Can you ...?

Recording 5

Okay, number one, we're one centimetre taller in the morning than in the evening ... yes, that's actually true! Isn't that strange! Number two, yes, this one's true. We can live about sixty days without food, which is about two months ... quite a long time really. Number three ... an adult eats about 200 kilos of food every year ... no actually that's wrong! Actually it's 500 kilos ... adults eat about 500 kilos of food every year! Number four, our bodies are about 70% water ... yes, that one's true too. Number five, yes this one is very strange but it's true! A baby really does have 306 bones in its body and an adult only two hundred and six ... they join together so two bones become one! Erm number six ... 50 per cent of your bones are in your hands and feet ... yes again that's true ... amazing isn't it?

Er, what's next? Yes, number seven, we can live without water for about twelve days ... no, that's not true, we can only live without water for about five to seven days. Number eight, this is amazing, I think! But yes, it's true ... every litre of blood that our bodies make travels 90,000 kilometres! Number nine ... a new baby can't see colours. Yes, that's true ... a new baby can see black and white and sometimes red. OK, and finally, number ten – an adult can see 10,000 different colours yes that's also true, I think that's incredible, too!

Recording 6

1 a second, a minute, an hour, a day

2 a centimetre, a metre, a kilometre

3 a gram, a kilo

4 1%   25%   80%   100%

Recording 7

P = Presenter J = Jack Warren A = Audience

P: ... and now it's time for you to put your questions to Jack. We only have two or three minutes so let's have the first question. Yes ... the lady over there

A1: How many people live on the Space Shuttle, Jack?

JW: Erm ... Sometimes there are four people, sometimes seven.

P: Okay, and the next question ... yes, please ...

A2: Where do you sleep?

JW: There aren't any beds, so we sleep in special sleeping bags.

A2: And erm another question about sleep ... when do you sleep?

JW: There is no night or day in space, so we sleep when it's nighttime in America.

P: Oh, that's interesting. Okay, we don't have much time so another question ... yes, the person there ...

A3: What can you do in your free time?

JW: We play cards, read books or sometimes we go for a spacewalk!

P: Wow! That sounds amazing! Okay ... and the lady there yes, you madam.

A4: Who do you talk to on Earth?

JW: Well of course we talk to the people at NASA every day, and sometimes we can talk to our families ... that's great!

P: And the very last question. Yes, madam.

A5: Why do you like working in space?

JW: Um, good question! Well ... because it's a very interesting job of course ... and, well, it's very beautiful up there, you know...

P: Okay, well we have to finish there now. So thank you very much to Jack Warren, and thank you very much at home...goodbye!

Recording 9

a) a hundred

b) three hundred

c) a hundred and fifty

d) two hundred and seventy-five

e) a thousand

f) twenty thousand

Recording 10

1 seven million

2 five thousand

3 eight hundred

4 one thousand two hundred

5 four hundred and seventy-five

6 six hundred and fifty thousand

7 three hundred and six

8 Nine thousand, nine hundred and ninety-nine

Consolidation modules 5–8, recording 1

A = Alice T = Tony

A: Who's Max?

T: Oh, he's a really good friend, but he doesn't usually write emails. He hates computers!

A: Where's he from?

T: Well, ... he's English, but now he lives in a place called Izmir, in Turkey.

A: Oh, right. What does he do there?

T: He works in a language school ... he's a teacher – he teaches English to Turkish students, adults and children.

A: Oh, interesting. And does he like living in Turkey?

T: Yes, he loves it there. He says that the people are really friendly, and the weather's great.

A: Lucky thing. So how do you know him?

T: Our parents live in the same street.

A: Oh, okay. So he's an old friend.

T: Yeah ... same school and everything. He's twenty-nine, the same age as me.

A: So what does he say in his email?

T: Well, he lives in a big flat near the school with two other teachers, and ... he goes to concerts a lot. Max loves all different kinds of music, especially jazz, and he can play the guitar really well.

A: Uh huh ... is he married?

T: Er ... no, he's not.

A: And can he cook?

T: Yes, he loves cooking, especially Italian food. His mother's Italian, you see.

A: Hmm ... maybe I'll go to Izmir for my holidays this year ...

Consolidation modules 5–8, recording 2

Eight days a week
Ooh, I need your love babe,
Guess you know it's true.
Hope you need my love babe,
Just like I need you.
Hold me, love me, hold me, love me.
Ain't got nothin' but love babe,
Eight days a week.

Love you ev'ry day girl,
Always on my mind.
One thing I can say girl,
Love you all the time.
Hold me, love me, hold me, love me.
Ain't got nothin' but love babe,
Eight days a week.

Eight days a week
I love you.
Eight days a week,
Is not enough to show I care.
Ooh, I need your love babe, ...
Eight days a week ...
Love you ev'ry ...
Eight days a week. Eight days a week. Eight days a week.

Module 9

Recording 1

young ... old
poor ... rich
new ... old
busy ... quiet
happy ... unhappy
slow ... fast
beautiful ... ugly
dangerous ... safe

Recording 2

1 In 1900 there were only about 9,000 cars in the world. Today there are about 650 million.

2 There were telephones and radios in 1900. The first telephone was in 1876, and the first radio was in 1895.

3 The journey across the Atlantic from New York to Europe was really quite fast in 1900. On a fast ship it was about six days.

4 There were about one a half billion people in the world in 1900. Today there are about six billion.

5 Most women were housewives in 1900 and a lot of women were also servants. There weren't many women with other jobs.

6 There were some women at university, but not many. For example at Oxford University in 1900 there were less than 200 women. Today there are more than 7,000 women.

7 Both California and Florida were part of the USA in 1900. All fifty states were in the USA by 1900.

8 Vienna was the capital of the Austrian Empire, and so it was very important in 1900. Hollywood was a small village near Los Angeles.

9 Moscow wasn't the capital of Russia. The capital was St Petersburg.

10 Abraham Lincoln wasn't the President of the United States in 1900, he was president more than forty years before that, from 1861–1865. The president in 1900 was William McKinley.

Recording 3

1 The President of the United States in 1900 was William McKinley.

2 Queen Victoria was the Queen of England, and Nicolas II was the Tsar of Russia.

3 There weren't many cars in the world, but bicycles were very popular. In Britain for example, there were 600,000 bicycles in 1900!

4 Cars were very slow. Roads weren't very good, and driving wasn't always safe.

5 Coca-Cola was a popular drink in America, but it wasn't well-known in other countries.

6 There were a lot of trains, but there weren't any aeroplanes. The first aeroplane was in 1907.

Recording 6

1900 1950 1990 1995 1984 1999 2000 2002 2005

Recording 7

a) 1995 b) 2008 c) 1949 d) 1906 e) 1899 f) 2020 g) 1918 h) 1980

Recording 8

a) Walt Disney was born in Chicago in 1901.
b) Catherine Zeta-Jones was born in Wales in 1969.
c) Mother Teresa was born in Skopje, in the Balkans, in 1910.
d) Luciano Pavarotti was born in Italy in 1935.
e) Al Pacino was born in New York in 1940.
f) Iman was born in Somalia in 1955.
g) Nicole Kidman was born in Hawaii in 1967.
h) Muhammad Ali was born in Louisville in 1942.

Module 10

Recording 1

1 Vincent van Gogh was born in Holland in 1853. Before he became a painter he sold pictures in an art gallery in The Hague. In 1886 he went to live with his brother, Theo, in Paris. When he was in France Van Gogh painted over 750 pictures, including *Sunflowers* and *Irises*. He was very poor, and only sold one painting in his life – but in 1990 someone sold his painting, *Portrait of Dr Gachet*, for eighty-two million dollars!

2 Bob Marley was born in Jamaica in 1945. His mother was Jamaican, and his father was English. Bob made his first album *Catch a Fire* in 1972, and his reggae music soon became famous all over the world. In 1975 he met his wife Rita at a concert, and

soon she became a singer in his band, The Wailers. Bob Marley died of cancer in 1981, but Rita and his son Ziggy still make reggae records today.

3   Coco Chanel was born in 1883, in France. She was from a poor French family and went to work in a hat shop when she was young. The clothes she made became popular in the 1920s. In 1920, she created the perfume, Chanel No. 5. She became a very rich and successful businesswoman

4   Charlie Chaplin was born in London in 1889. In 1912 he left England and went to work as an actor in Hollywood. He made his first film in 1914, and soon became very famous. In 1920 his salary was $10,000 a week! In 1952 Charlie Chaplin left the USA, and went to live in Switzerland. In his life he made over 100 films, and he had four wives and twelve children. Charlie Chaplin died on Christmas Day in 1977.

Recording 2

leave ... left	write ... wrote
sell ... sold	become ... became
go ... went	make ... made
meet ... met	have ... had

Recording 3

1   John Lennon sang with the Beatles and wrote songs.
2   Shakespeare wrote *Romeo and Juliet*
3   Billie Holiday sang blues and jazz.
4   Elvis Presley was an actor and a singer.
5   Audrey Hepburn was an actress.
6   Mozart wrote operas.

Recording 9

a)   A: What's the date today?
     B: Er ... it's the twenty-first, I think.
b)   A: When's your birthday?
     B: April the fifteenth.
c)   John Lennon was born on October the ninth, 1940.
d)   I was born on December the thirtieth.
e)   My parents got married on January the sixteenth, 1982.
f)   I met my husband on March the twelfth. It was a cold day, and I was ...

Module 11

Recording 1

A = Annette M = Matt
A: Hello, Matt, how are you?
M: Oh, I'm fine, thanks.
A: I didn't see you last week.
M: No, Claire and I went to New York on holiday.
A: Oh, wow! What did you do there?
M: Oh, lots of things. The first day we went for a walk in Manhattan. It was very busy, lots of buildings and cars. Then on the second day we ... er ... went shopping, and went to one or two museums. The Metropolitan Museum was closed, though, so we didn't go there.
A: Did you go to the Statue of Liberty?
M: Yes, of course. We went to the top, and you can see all of New York from there – it looks fantastic! But we didn't go to the Empire State Building. Next time, maybe.
A: Did you stay in a hotel?
M: No, we didn't, we stayed with friends. They lived on 9th Avenue, near Central Park. We were lucky they live there, because New York's a really expensive city.
A: Hmmm. So what was the best place you went to?
M: Er ... Central Park, I think. We went for a walk there every day. It's a beautiful park, very big, and it's interesting watching all the

people there.
A: What about the food?
M: Oh, we ate sandwiches and burgers all the time! We didn't go to expensive restaurants, because we didn't have a lot of money.
A: So you had a good time then.
M: Oh, yes, it was great. We want to go back again next year.
A: Hmmm. I think I need a holiday ...

Recording 2

a)   They went for a walk in Manhattan.
b)   They went shopping.
c)   They didn't go to the Metropolitan Museum.
d)   They went to the Statue of Liberty.
e)   They didn't go to the Empire State Building.
f)   They didn't stay in a hotel.
g)   They stayed with friends.
h)   They went for a walk in Central Park.

Recording 3

1   Did you have a nice holiday?
2   What did you do last Sunday?
3   Did you go out last night?
4   Did you have a nice weekend?
5   Did you watch TV last night?

Recording 4

last year   last month   last weekend   yesterday   last night this morning

Recording 7

V = Veronica T = Ticket seller
V: Can I have a return to Oxford, please?
T: Okay, that's ... er ... £23.50.
V: Here you are. What time's the next train?
T: Well, there's one at ... 10.54.
V: Oh, good. Which platform?
T: Platform ... sixteen.
V: Okay, thanks a lot. Bye.

Module 12

Recording 1

a carpet   a book   coffee   a magazine   jeans   a jacket   a car boots   clothes   make-up   shampoo   a mobile phone

Recording 2

a, things you carry with you
a handbag, a briefcase
b, things you wear
a jumper, shoes, a T-shirt,
c, things in the house
a chair, a table, a lamp

Recording 3

a)   **Yuko**: I want to buy a CD this weekend – the new Bon Jovi CD – and I want some new shoes for work too.
b)   **Antonia**: Nothing! I don't want to buy anything this weekend – I don't want to go near any shops – it's too hot! I want to go to the beach and relax!
c)   **Ali**: I want a new leather jacket. There's a really nice one in a shop near school ... but it's very expensive!
d)   **Lucas**: I want a lamp for my bedroom – something really nice ... blue ... or maybe green ... something that's different ...

Recording 4

a) A: What colour is it?
   B: Yellow.
b) A: How much is it?
   B: $125
c) A: What size is it?
   B: Medium.

Recording 5

a)
My mother's in hospital so I'm going to visit her this afternoon, and I want to take her some flowers.
b)
After lunch we're going to visit the castle museum, and then we're going to find a hotel.
c)
I'm not going to buy a computer today, but I want to look at some different models, then I can think about them ...
d)
I'm going to meet my girlfriend's parents this evening – we're going to have dinner at their house.

Recording 6

1 My mother's in hospital, so I'm going to visit her this afternoon.
2 We're going to visit the Castle Museum. Then we're going to find a hotel.
3 I'm not going to buy a computer today.
4 I'm going to meet my girlfriend's parents this evening. We're going to have dinner at their house.

Recording 7

1 A: Are you going to phone Linda today?
   B: No, she's going to phone me.
2 A: Are you going to drive to the airport tomorrow?
   B: I'm going to take the bus, I think.
3 A: Are you going to go out tonight?
   B: No, I'm going to watch that Woody Allen film on TV ... I'm really tired.
4 A: Are you going to go to the shops this morning?
   B: Yes, soon. Do you want something?
5 A: Are you going to have a holiday this year?
   B: Yes, I think we're going to stay with my aunt and uncle in London.
6 A: What are you going to do when you finish university?
   B: I don't know. I think I'm going to work with my father.

Recording 8

1 Are you going to phone Linda today?
2 Are you going to go out tonight?
3 No. I'm going to watch TV.

Recording 9

a) A: Good luck with your new job!
   B: Thanks.
b) A: Have a nice weekend!
   B: Thank you, you too.
c) A: Good luck with your new school!
   B: Thank you very much.
d) A: Have a nice holiday!
   B: Thanks, and you!
e) A: See you in September!
   B: Yes, see you – have a nice holiday!

Consolidation modules 9–12, recording 1

When I was young I lived in Scotland, in a village near the sea. Life was very different then. It was the 1930s, so there wasn't any TV, but my family had a radio, and we listened to it every evening. My parents didn't have a car, so I went to school by bicycle – six miles every day! But I didn't study very hard, and left school when I was fourteen. There weren't any cinemas near our village, so every Saturday I met my friends on the beach and we played football all day. When I was fifteen my parents sold our house and the family moved to England. I never went back to my village, but I can still hear the sea in my head ...

Consolidation modules 9–12, recording 3

Money, Money, Money
I work all night, I work all day, to pay the bills I have to pay
Ain't it sad?
And still there never seems to be a single penny left for me
That's too bad.
In my dreams I have a plan,
If I got me a wealthy man,
I wouldn't have to work at all, I'd fool around and have a ball ...

Money, money, money
Must be funny
In the rich man's world.
Money, money, money
Always sunny
In the rich man's world.
Aha-ahaaa
All the things I could do
If I had a little money,
It's a rich man's world.

A man like that is hard to find but I can't get him off my mind
Ain't it sad?
And if he happens to be free I bet he wouldn't fancy me,
That's too bad.
So I must leave, I'll have to go,
To Las Vegas or Monaco,
And win a fortune in a game – my life will never be the same ...

Money, money, money
Must be funny
In the rich man's world.
Money, money, money
Always sunny
In the rich man's world.
Aha-ahaaa
All the things I could do
If I had a little money,
It's a rich man's world.

Author acknowledgements

We would like to thank everyone at Pearson Education for all their input, encouragement and advice, particularly Frances Woodward and Jenny Colley (Senior Publishers), Sarah Hounsell (Senior Designer), Judith Walters and Naomi Tasker (Senior Editors), Alma Gray and Andrew Branch (Producers), Andrew Thorpe (Mac Artist).

The publishers and authors are very grateful to the following people and institutions for reporting on the manuscript: Gözde Alkan, Yeditepe University, Turkey; Mariella Ansaldo, Liceo Scientifico Statale "G D Cassini", Genoa; Robert Armitage, IH, Company Training, Barcelona; Helen Bain, IH, Suadiye, Istanbul; Jacqueline Cook, IH, Serrano, Madrid; Rosemary Evans, Dubai Men's College; Yvonne Gobert, The Chamber of Commerce, Chartres; Simon Green, British Council, Istanbul; Sarah Hartley, Merit School, Barcelona; Tim Hood, British Council, Istanbul; Claire Jaynes, EF International School of English, London; Rachel Kirsch, Hammersmith & West London College; Alison Knowles, IH, Buenos Aires; Colin Mackenzie, Langage Forum, Courbevoie La Defense, Paris; Nicola Marsden, Higher College of Technology, Abu Dhabi, UAE; Michael O'Brien; British Council, Milan; Hülya Onay, Marmara University – School of Foreign Languages, Istanbul; Giuseppe Picone, Civici Corsi Serali – di Lingue Straniere, Milan; Ewa Spirydowocz, Archibald School and VII LO im J. Slowackiego, Warsaw; Ewa Sobczak, English Unlimited, Gdansk; Naciye Türe, Marmara University – School of Foreign Languages, Istanbul.

Chris Redston would like to thank the following people for their help and contribution: Mark and Laura Skipper, Dylan Evans, Joss Whedon, Polly Kirby, Margie Baum.

We are grateful to the following for permission to reproduce copyright material:

Bocu Music Limited for lyrics of *Money, Money, Money*, recorded by Abba; and Sony/ATV Music Publishing (UK) Limited for lyrics of *Eight Days a Week* and *Hello, Goodbye* recorded by The Beatles.

Illustrated by: Melanie Barnes, Kathy Baxendale, Graham Berry (The Art Collection), Paul Burgess, Rebecca Gibbon (The Inkshed), Andy Hammond (Illustration Ltd), Sarah McMenemy (The Artworks), Toby Morison (Heart), Robert Nelmes (The Organisation), David Newton (Début Art), David Smith (The Organisation), Jane Smith, Andy Walker (Artist Partners).

Photo acknowledgements

The publishers would like to thank the following for their permission to reproduce copyright photographs.

Art Directors & Trip for pages 8 (a, c & d), 16 (top left), 17 (c, d & e), 18 (30, 50 & 90), 35 (bottom), 40 (5), 54, 57 (bottom), 68 (background & top), 74 (top right & left), 75 (top), 78 (top right), 82 (bottom middle), 84 (middle left), 88 (bottom right) 95 (bottom left, middle and right), 100 bottom (middle bottom); Andes Press for page 48 (e); Anthony Blake Photo Library for page 26 (a, b, c, d, f, h, i, k and l); Corbis Images for pages 18 (b), 64 (1), 78 top left, 82 middle top, 85, 95 top left; Corbis Stock Market for pages 26 (g), 41, 58 (top), 68 (bottom), 75 (bottom), 90 left and right; Sarah Cunningham for page 40 (2); James Davies for page 22 (a); DK for page 26 (j), 30 (c & e); Greg Evans for pages 8 (h), 17 (a), 18 (c), 19 (d, e & h), 19 (bottom), 24 (top), 26 (e), 50 (left & right), 59 (top right), 67, 68 (bottom left), 90 right (inset); 72 (top left); Mary Evans Picture Library for pages 74 (middle), 76 (bottom & top right), 77 (top), 79; FPG International for page 10; Format Photographers for page 59 (bottom); Hulton Getty for pages 40 (4), 74 (bottom), 75 (middl) 76 (middle & top left), 77 (middle & bottom), 78 (middle), 82 (left & right), 106; Hutchison Picture Library for pages 8 (f), 30 (d); Image Bank for page 59 bottom (inset); Image State for pages 23 (e), 25 (top x 2), 72 (bottom left), 88 (top right), 94; Impact for pages 64 (3), 78 (top left), 88 (left & top right), 89, 91 (top & bottom); Life File Photographic Library for page 34 (inset); Magnum for page 30 (b); Moviestore Collection for page 48 (a); Panos Pictures for pages 22 (b & c), 58 (bottom right), 65 (bottom); Pearson Education/James Walker for page 6 (all), 20, 25 (middle & bottom), 28 , 29, 45 (all), 46, 52, 53, 54, 62 (all), 97, 100 (top), 110 (top left & bottom left), 108 (middle left & top middle right), 109; The Photographers Library for page 35 top (inset) and 35 bottom (inset); Picturebank for page 23 (d); Popperfoto for page 84 (top & bottom right); Powerstock for pages 17 (b), 18 (f), 24 (bottom), 40 (3), 70; Redferns for pages 48 (c), 83 (top left & top right); Rex Features for pages 8 (b), 9 (6, a & b), 9a, b, c, & d), 16 (bottom right & middle right), 18 (a), 19 (g), 30 (f), 34, 40 (1), 48 (d), 57 (top & bottom), 80 (all), 83 (bottom right, middle top, bottom left & middle bottom), 84 (left); Science Photo Library for pages 8 (e & g), 68 (bottom right); SIPA Press for page 58 (left); Spectrum for page 30 (a), 35 top; Sporting Pictures for pages 9 (6c & d), 16 (bottom left & top right), 64 (2) and 64 (4); Stone for 72 (right); Telegraph Colour Library for pages 65 (top & middle); Alaister Thain/PG for page 16 (middle left); Janine Wiedel for pages 17 (f), 18 (20, 40, 60, 70, 80 & 100), 19 (top), 59 (top), 61, 100 bottom (middle top, right & left), 108 (top, bottom, bottom right), 110 (top right, middle & bottom),

The photograph on page 59 left has been kindly supplied by Peter Holly.

We are grateful to Allied Carpets, Russell & Bromley and Sendo for pages 98-99 and 109 and to the BBC, BMW, DKNY, EMI, IBM and KLM for permission to reproduce their logos on page 10. Thanks also to Harlow Town Station and Bell College, Saffron Walden for their help with the commissioned photography.

The cover photograph has been kindly supplied by Bruce Coleman Collection.

Freelance picture research by: Jacqui Rivers and Liz Moore
Commissioned photography by: James Walker

150989